How to Pray in Islam

A Comprehensive Guide to Performing Salah and Understanding Why Prayer Is Important

Manuscript 1

How to Pray Salah

A Step-By-Step Guide to Connecting with Your Creator Through Islamic Prayer

Table of Contents

Introduction

In the Name of Allah, the Most Gracious, the Most Merciful, and by His blessing, we begin our book on Salah. May Allah (SWT) guide us and you to do good and honest deeds and to Jannah in the Hereafter.

Salah is the center of Islam. It is the second pillar of the Islamic faith, following the two Shahadahs (professions that There is no God but Allah and that Muhammad, May Peace Be Upon Him, is the messenger and servant of Allah). It is also the first thing a Muslim is asked about on the Day of Judgement. Prophet Muhammad (PBUH) is reported to say: *"The first of man's deeds for which he will be called to account on the Day of Resurrection will be Salah. If it is found to be perfect, he will be safe and successful; but if it is incomplete, he will be unfortunate and a loser."* Prophet Muhammad (PBUH) is also reported to say: *"Verily, between a man and unbelief, is abandoning the Salah."* Salah is when a Muslim goes out of their way five times a day, every day, to connect with their Creator, Allah (SWT).

Salah symbolizes the complete submission of a Muslim's will to Allah (SWT), especially in Sujud (prostration in English). Salah is mentioned in the Qur'an many times;

however, it was taught by the Prophet Muhammad (PBUH). Let's also remember that Salah is not a chore but a connection with Allah (SWT) and a shield from hellfire. So, let's learn about how to prepare for Salah.

Chapter 1: How to Prepare for Salah

First and foremost is intention; intention to perform Salah for Allah (SWT). We must all remember that Salah is not just a charade or series of movements performed a certain number of times. It is a period when you are standing in front of Allah (SWT), our one and only Creator. This calls for honesty in intention and truth in action. You don't pray Salah just because it is a mandatory prayer, but in seeking Allah's (SWT) satisfaction of Allah (SWT) and because it provides an escape from the hassle of daily life. It was narrated that Abu Ayyub said: "A man came to the Prophet (PBUH) and said: 'O Messenger of Allah, teach me and make it concise.' Muhammad (PBUH) responded: 'When you stand to pray, pray like a man bidding farewell. Do not say anything for which you will have to apologize. And give up hope for what other people have.' During Salah, you must concentrate on what truly matters; you must pray Salah with Khushu' (Reverence in English), for you are standing before Allah Almighty (SWT). Let's start with the first step, Wudu'.

Wudu'

Wudu' is the purification or ablution required by all Muslims before performing all Salawat (plural of Salah). Performing Wudu' is very simple.

1. *There is a certain process to ablution that is required before every prayer. Source: https://commons.wikimedia.org/wiki/File:Ablution_tap_in_Al-Ittihad_Mosque.JPG*

2. Intention

The first step is intention (niyyah in Arabic). We've also mentioned intention before, but why is it so important? Umar ibn al-Khattab reported that Prophet Muhammad (PBUH) said: "Deeds are but with intentions, and for the man is only what he intended. So, one whose emigration was to Allah and His Messenger (PBUH), then his emigration was to Allah and His Messenger (PBUH), and whoever emigrated to worldly benefits or to a woman to marry, his emigration would be to what he emigrated for." Good deeds aren't really good if they're not meant well, are they? For example, two people could spend their money feeding the poor. One intends his actions to please and satisfy Allah (SWT), and the other intends to show how good of a person they are. Whom do you think Allah (SWT) considers better? Therefore, it is important to be mindful during Wudu' and intend to do it for the sake of Allah (SWT).

3. In the Name of Allah the Most Gracious, the Most Merciful

After that, you should say, *"Bismillah Ar-Rahman Ar-Raheem,"* which means, "In the Name of Allah the Most Gracious the Most Merciful." Ideally, we should be saying this before all of our actions, for this is a very commendable act, as Prophet Muhammad (PBUH) is reported to say to Umar ibn Abi Salamah: "Mention Allah's Name (i.e., say Bismillah)." Saying *"Bismillah Ar-Rahman Ar-Raheem"* is fine out loud or silently in your heart. It also serves as an initiation for the purification of Wudu'.

4. Wash Your hands

It is a Sunnah (practice) of the Prophet Muhammad (PBUH) to wash his hands before Wudu'. It is optional to wash them once, twice, or thrice, although it is preferable to wash them three times. Start by washing your right hand thoroughly three times. Make sure the water reaches every part of your hand, leaving no dry spots. This includes removing anything on the skin like mud, nail polish, or anything similar that blocks the water from your skin or fingernails. After thoroughly washing your right hand, wash your left hand, preferably thrice as well, in the same manner, covering the spaces between your fingers and the nails.

5. Rinse Your Mouth Thrice

Now, for the first 'official' step of Wudu.' Cup your right hand and put some water in it. Then, rinse your mouth with this water. Move the water well around your mouth to cleanse it properly, and then spit it out. Do this three times.

6. Blow Your Nose Thrice

After that, take some water into your right hand and sniff it into your nostrils. Then, blow the water out. Do this three times, as well. The word 'sniff' is the closest translation of the word Istinshaq in Arabic. You could think of it as blowing your nose with a handful of water.

7. Wash Your Face Thrice

In this step, similar to washing your hands, nothing must cover your face. You must wash your entire face. From the top of your forehead to the bottom of your chin and from one ear to another. Not the ears themselves, though; these are in a later step. For men with a beard, run your fingers through your beard to wash it as you wash your face. Do this three times.

8. Wash Your Arms Thrice

Starting at your fingertips, wash your arms all the way to your elbows. Start with your right and then your left. Do this three times. Make sure your whole forearm and hand are all washed carefully, leaving no dry spots.

9. Wipe Your Head Once

Notice here that this step doesn't require full washing. You only need to wipe your head with your wet hands from the crown of your head – the highest point of the forehead – to the back of your head – right at the beginning of the back of your neck - and then return your hands from the back of your head to the crown again; one wipe back, and one wipe forward. Do this once. For people with long hair, as implied in the beginning, it is not necessary to ruffle the hair or wash it entirely. You only need to wipe your head from the crown to the bottom. It is narrated that Prophet Muhammad (PBUH) when doing Wudu', wiped his entire head from the crown to the back of the head without disturbing the hair. So, if your hair is long and you wish not to ruffle it, you may wipe from the crown of your head to the back without bringing your hands back.

10.   Wash Your Ears Once

Use your thumbs and index fingers to clean the outside and the inside of your ears with the same water you wiped your head with in the last step. You only need to do this once.

11. Wash Your Feet Thrice

For the final step, start at your toes and wash your feet from there to your ankle bones. Wash between the toes, the back of the ankle, and the heels; carefully wash your entire foot. Do this three times with your right foot and then three times with your left, making sure you leave no dry spots like before.

12. I Bear Witness

Now, you have completed your Wudu'. Following the Sunnah of the Prophet Muhammad (PBUH), you should say, *"Ash-hadu allaa ilaha illallah wa ash-hadu anna Muhammadan 'abduhu wa Rasuluh,"* this means "I Bear Witness that there is no God but Allah, and I bear witness that Muhammad is His servant and messenger."

After that, the Prophet (PBUH) would say the following Dua' (prayer i.e., asking Allah (SWT) for something): *"Allahuma j'alnee minat-tawwabeen waj'alnee minal mutatahireen,"* which means "O Allah, make me among those who seek repentance and make me among those who purify themselves." Now, you are ready to pray.

What Nullifies Wudu'

Now you might ask: "Should I do this before every Salah? How long does my Wudu' last?" The answer to this is simple. Wudu' is only nullified – i.e., you have to renew your Wudu' to pray – by the following things:

- Any natural discharge of the body: urine, stool, or passing gas.
- Falling asleep.
- Losing consciousness.
- Ejaculation; for both men and women.

A minor note: let's say you do wudu' before one prayer, and you pray the said prayer. Then, you stay until the time of the following prayer without meeting any of the nullifiers of Wudu'. You may go to pray directly. In other words, you don't have to do Wudu' before every Salah. One wudu' could last with you to two prayers, or three, or maybe all five of the day if you don't meet any of the above-mentioned nullifiers.

Wudu' with Socks or Shoes on

Let's say you did Wudu' once, and then you had to redo your Wudu', but this time you have socks on. You don't have to take them off. The sole difference is in step #10 (washing your feet). When you have your socks on during Wudu', instead of washing your feet three times, you gently wipe the top of your right foot with your right hand and then the same for your left foot, both with your right hand and over the sock. This applies to shoes or sandals as well, as long as they cover up to the ankles.

Note on Dressing

Salah is when a Muslim goes to stand before Allah (SWT), so it is preferable and commendable to wear the best clothes one has. Allah (SWT) says in Surah Al-A'raf chapter 7, verse 31 of the Holy Qur'an: "O Sons of Adam! Take your adornment at every mosque." Allah (SWT) urges his devoted worshippers to dress well when going to pray in mosques. However, you do not have to be formally dressed in a suit and tie or such. As for coverage, the Prophet Muhammad (PBUH) has instructed that men should be covered from the naval to the knee and preferably wear something that covers their shoulders. So, although not forbidden, tank tops are not preferable during Salah. Women, on the other hand, must cover all their bodies except the hands and the face.

Where to Pray

The place of prayer must be clean. You can pray on grass, sand, concrete, etc. If the place isn't clean, you can use a carpet or a prayer rug to cover the area where you will be praying. Mind that the place should not be too noisy or have too many people around. Try choosing a quiet and peaceful place. For example, if the time of prayer comes and you are sitting with your whole family in the living room with the TV on, you should go into a quieter room and get ready for your Salah. This allows for better Khushu', as distractions around you always take away your focus.

After finding a quiet place, face the Qiblah. From your location, the Qiblah of Islam is the direction of Kaa'bah in Makkah. Allah (SWT) commanded this directly in the Qur'an in Surah al-Baqarah chapter 2 verse, and He says: "We have already seen the turning about of your face to the heaven; so, We will indeed definitely turn you towards a Qiblah that shall satisfy you. So, turn your face towards the Sacred Mosque (the Mosque the Kaa'bah sits at the center of in Makkah), and (O Muslims), wherever you are, turn your faces in its direction."

When to Pray

In Islam, there are five daily mandatory prayers (Al-Salawat Al-Fara'id in Arabic). First is Fajr, prayed before dawn. Second is Dhuhr, prayed at noon. After that is Asr, prayed in the afternoon when an object's shadow is exactly as long as the object is. Maghrib comes next, prayed at sunset. Finally, Isha' is prayed at nightfall. Nowadays, calendars have precise timings on them, so you don't have to worry about following the sun's position and measuring shadows.

Chapter 2: Understanding the Components of Salah

Now that we're ready for Salah and facing the Qiblah, let's learn its components and the movements done during Salah. Salah is very simple. In this chapter, we'll discuss the positions you have to assume in Salah individually to clarify them. The actual steps will be discussed in the next chapter. This chapter will describe the positions in the same order they are supposed to be performed in Salah to better grasp the essence of the different movements. We will start with the physical movements, then the recitations, and then we'll put them together in the following chapter Insha'Allah.

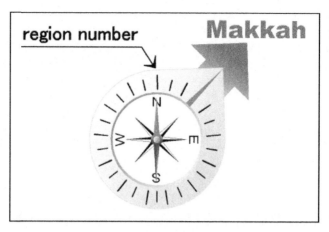

2. To ensure you're facing Makkah, it's important to use a qibla compass. Source: https://commons.wikimedia.org/wiki/File:Qibla_compass.png

---

Takbirat al Ihram

When you are standing, facing the Qiblah, of course, you raise your hands to the side of your head, preferably up to your ear lobes, and say "Allahu Akbar," meaning Allah (SWT) is The Greatest. This is called Takbirat al Ihram.

3. Takbirat al Ihram position. Source: https://unsplash.com/photos/PXYJRuXC2Vg

---

This way, you've started your Salah.

Qiyam

This is the posture of standing. You stand after saying Takbirat al Ihram with your hands folded over each other, the right always above the left, on your chest, and your eyes looking down at the ground at an angle. Remember not to look straight down; look at where your forehead will be during Sujud. Sujud will be explained shortly Insha'Allah. Your legs don't have to be too tight or too wide; they should be shoulder-width, or a little tighter is also good.

Ruku'

In this position, you are bending over with your back and arms straight and your palms on your knees, bowing essentially. Most people have their fingers pointing to their sides wrapped around their knees; however, pointing your fingers down at your feet is preferable.

Qaumah

Qaumah is the same as Qiyam. You stand back up after Ruku'. Before Ruku', you must have your hands folded on your chest. After Ruku', you can leave them at your sides or fold them on your chest; it is optional.

Sujud

After getting back up from Ruku and finishing your Qaumah, you go down to the ground performing Sujud. In Sujud, you bow low on the ground with both your hands and your knees touching the floor and your forehead and nose. Your toes should also be on the ground. The Prophet Muhammad (PBUH) has been reported to say: "When one of you prostrates, he should not kneel in the manner of a camel but should put down his hands before his knees." So, be careful to let your hands touch the ground before your knees do. Also, make sure that your toes touch the ground, as this is an essential part of prostration; Sujud is invalid without it. It is preferred if you can bend your toes under your feet, pointing them in the direction of the Qiblah, as this was the Sunnah of the Prophet Muhammad (PBUH). Remember not to let your forearms rest on the ground; for this position is similar to a dog sitting on the ground; your elbows should be at your sides, as Anas ibn Malik, one of the trusty companions of the Prophet (PBUH) has narrated that the Prophet Muhammad (PBUH) said: "Be straight in the prostrations and none of you should put his forearms on the ground (in the prostration) like a dog."

Juluus

Juluus, in Arabic, means sitting. In this position, you are simply sitting on the ground with your legs folded under you and your hands laying palms down at the ends of your thighs above your knees. The way your feet are positioned is up to you. You can keep both feet upright and sit on the backs of your heels with the balls of your feet on the ground supporting you. This is a valid way to sit. Following the Sunnah of the Prophet (PBUH), the better way is to keep your right foot upright with toes bent pointing at the Qiblah, lay your left foot under you, and sit on it. The second way, the one with the right foot upright and the left foot laid down, is the way the Prophet Muhammad (PBUH) sat most of the time, so it is best practice to do as he (PBUH) did. Both positions are with your knees in front of you and your feet under you; the only difference is the positioning of the feet. This covers all the physical positions you must assume during your Salah to Allah (SWT). Now, let's go over what you have to recite during Salah.

Reciting the Holy Qur'an

First and foremost, you start by reciting chapter 1 of the Holy Qur'an, Surah al-Fatihah. It is a Sunnah of the Prophet Muhammad (PBUH) to say *"A'uthu billahi min ashaitan irrajeem"* which means "I seek protection in Allah from Shaytan (the devil), the accursed one." before reciting Al-Fatihah, this is called Ta'awwudh. After Ta'awwudh, you do Tasmiyah, mentioning the name of Allah Almighty, by saying *"Bismillahir Rahmanir Raheem."* After that, you recite the seven Holy verses of Surah al-Fatihah, and then you say "Ameen":

"Al hamdu lil lahi rabbil 'alamin. Arrahmanir Rahim. Maliki yawmiddin. Iyyaka na'budu wa iyyaka nasta'in. Ihdinas siratal mustaqim. Siratal ladhina an'amta'alaihim, ghairil maghdubi'alaihim walad dhallin. (Ameen)"

Translation in English:

"All praises and thanks to Allah, the Lord of the worlds, the most Gracious, the most Merciful; Master of the Day of Judgment. You alone we worship; from You alone, we seek help. Guide us along the straight path – the path of those You favored, not those who earned Your anger or went astray."

You must recite Surah al-Fatihah in all Rak'ah of your Salah. Rak'ah will be shortly explained Insha'Allah.

After reciting Al-Fatihah, you recite any other passage from the Holy Qur'an. This differs between some Rak'ah and others, but this will also be explained shortly Insha'Allah. The length of the passage you recite is up to you; you could read three short verses (Ayah), one long Ayah, or the entire Surah al-Baqarah in one Rak'ah. The most common practice is to read one short Surah. Here is one example of a short Surah you could read:

"Bismillah Al-Rahman Al-Raheem

Qul Huwa-Allahu Ahad, Allahu El-Samad, Lam yalid wa lam yulad, Wa lam ya kun lahu kufuwan ahad."

This is the 112th chapter of the Holy Qur'an, Surah al-Ikhlas.

Translation in English:

"In the name of Allah, the Most Gracious, the Most Merciful. Say, He is Allah, the One. Allah is Eternal and Absolute. He begets not, nor was He begotten. And there is none co-equal unto Him."

Saying *"Bismillah Ar-Rahman Ar-Raheem"* before reciting the short Surah is optional. All these Surahs are recited during Qiyam when you are standing up after you say Takbirat al-Ihram.

Rak'ah

Rak'ah are units of Salah. They differ between different Salawat (plural of Salah), and it would be easier to explain them each with their respective Salah. The main difference is in the number of Rak'ah and certain movements done at the end of the second Rak'ah and sometimes the third and the fourth. The next chapter will make all these actions clearer and show the remaining parts in detail as well. These include Tasbih, Tashahhud, Taslim, and how different prayers like Fajr, Dhuhr, Maghrib, and Isha are prayed.

Chapter 3: Step-by-step Guide to Performing Salah

You've completed your wudu' and learned the basics. Now is the time for Salah. Salah is performed five times a day with different numbers of Rak'ah. Fajr, before dawn, has two, Dhuhr and Asr have four, Maghrib has three, and Isha has four. Let's see how every Rak'ah should go, and we'll discuss them chronologically with how the five prayers should be prayed.

4. *Salah is performed in a specific way and the process is important to understand. Source: https://unsplash.com/photos/JHb1mRYJ11U*

So, the first Salah is Fajr, prayed before dawn.

Fajr

#1: Intention

We've mentioned this with Wudu' and mention it here again to emphasize it more. Prophet Muhammad (PBUH) has been reported to say: "Deeds are but with intentions." You must intend from your heart to pray to Allah (SWT) for His satisfaction. This part is important not only to the purity of the intention but to the validity of your Salah. Your entire focus should be on the prayer and utterly nothing else. This is what's called Khushu'.

#2: Takbirat al Ihram

We've discussed this briefly in the previous chapter. You stand upright facing the Qiblah, raise your hands beside your earlobes, and say *"Allahu Akbar,"* which means "Allah is the Greatest." Right now, your prayer has officially begun. As we mentioned before, it is important to focus solely and wholeheartedly on prayer and ignore distractions as much as possible.

#3: Qiyam

Qiyam, as mentioned in the previous chapter, is standing upright with your back straight and your hands folded over your chest. Remember: the right over the left. Start by reciting Dua' al-Thana':

"Subhaanaka Allaahumma wa bihamdika, watabarakasmuka, wa ta'ala jadduka, wa laa 'ilaaha ghayruka." This means: "Glory and praise be to You, O Allah. Blessed be Your name and exalted be Your majesty,

there is none worthy of worship except You." You say Dua' al-Thana' only in the first Rak'ah.

Then, following the Sunnah of the Prophet (PBUH), you should say al Ta'awwudh:

"A'uthu billahi minash shaitanir rajeem."

This means: "I seek protection in Allah from Shaytan (the devil), the accursed one." After that, you do Tasmiyah; say "Bismillahir Rahmanir Raheem," and you start reciting Surat al-Fatihah:

"Al hamdu lil lahi rabbil 'alamin. Arrahmanir rahim. Maliki yawmiddin. Iyyaka na'budu wa iyyaka nasta'in. Ihdinas siratal mustaqim. Siratal ladhina an'amta'alaihim, ghairil maghdubi'alaihim wa lad dhallin. (Ameen)"

The translation of this was mentioned Alhamdulillah in the previous chapter. If you are praying alone, you must recite al-Fatihah in every Rak'ah of every Salah, obligatory or not.

Also, if you are praying alone, it is preferable, in Fajr, to recite the verses of the Qur'an out loud as this is the Sunnah of the Prophet Muhammad (PBUH). If you are praying behind an Imam and he recites loudly, saying "Ameen" after the Imam finishes reciting Surah al-Fatihah is sufficient. One thing you must never do is recite loudly along with the Imam.

Now, after reciting Surah al-Fatihah, since we are in the first Rak'ah in Fajr, you follow it by reciting a passage from the Holy Qur'an. You read this out loud as well. Length is not constricted at all; reading one or two verses or a full chapter is totally up to you. For Rak'ah, in which you will be reciting a passage of the Qur'an after al-Fatihah, here is an example of a short chapter of the Holy Qur'an:

"Inna a'taynakal Kawthar, fasalli lirabbik wa inhar, inna shani'aka huwal abtar"

This is the full chapter 108 Surah al-Kawthar, the shortest chapter in the Book of Allah (SWT), and here it is in English:

"Surely we have given you the Abundance; So, pray to your Lord and slaughter (the sacrifice). Surely your antagonist is he who is without offspring (lit. curtailed)."

#4: Ruku'

After you finish reciting, say "Allahu Akbar" once more and bow down, assuming the position of Ruku'. Bow down, put your hands on your knees in the manner we described before, and *say "Subhana Rabbiyal Adhim"* three times. This means: "How Perfect is my Lord, the Supreme. When you bow down, look at the place where your forehead will be during Sujud and keep your head in line with your back.

#5: Get Back up

Get back up from Ruku' to standing up straight again. As you get up say *"Sami'Allahu liman hamidah."* This means: "Allah hears those who praise Him." After that, you say, "Rabbana wa lakal hamd," which means: "Our Lord, praise be to You." If you are praying behind an Imam when he says *"Sami'Allahu liman hamidah,"* you don't have to say it; you can just say "Rabbana wa lakal hamd" when you get up.

#6: Sujud

After you say *"Rabbana wa lakal hamd"* standing straight, you go down to prostrate on the floor and say *"Allahu Akbar"* as you go down to the floor. Remember to put your hands down on the floor before your knees as the Prophet (PBUH) has instructed. Also, remember the seven parts of the body that are to touch the floor: the forehead, nose, knees, toes, and palms of your hands. Remember to keep your forearms off the ground and your elbows at your sides. Then, you say *"Subhana Rabiyal A'la"* three times. This means: "How Perfect is my Lord, the Highest."

5. *Sujud. Source: https://www.pexels.com/photo/muslim-black-man-praying-at-home-5996991/*

Abu Hurayrah (may Allah be pleased with him), one of the closest companions of the Prophet Muhammad (PBUH), reported that the Prophet (PBUH) said: "The nearest a slave is to his Lord is when he is prostrating, so increase (your) supplications (while in this state)." Sujud is the best time to do Dua' (supplications), and Allah (SWT) says in Surah Ghafir chapter 40 verse 60: "And your Lord has said, "Invoke Me, and I will respond to you." This is the time for you to ask Allah (SWT) and remember He is the Most Generous and the Most Merciful.

#7: Juluus

After saying *"Subhana Rabiyal A'la"* three times, you get up from Sujud sitting on your left leg, as we discussed in the previous chapter. Your left foot rests on the floor, with your right foot upright and its toes pointing in the direction of the Qiblah. Don't forget to say *"Allahu Akbar"* on your way up. This is the Sunnah of the Prophet Muhammad (PBUH); however, it is OK if you wish to sit with both feet propped up. You place your hands, palms facing down near the end of your thighs, and you say, *"Rabbigh-fir lee,"* which means: "O my Lord, forgive me." You say this three times.

#8: Return to Sujud

After doing Juluus once, you go back down to the position of Sujud, like step #6, and say *"Subhana Rabiyal A'la"* three times and say your supplications if you wish. Now you have done Sujud twice and have completed your first Rak'ah. After your second Sajdah (the act of prostration means one prostration), you get back up to your feet, standing up straight with your hands folded on your chest, again right over left. Remember to say *"Allahu Akbar"* as you are getting up.

#9: The Second Rak'ah

After you've stood up, you start with Surah al-Fatihah again, just like the first Rak'ah, and you repeat all the previous steps except for Ta'awwudh and Dua' al-Thana'. After Surah al-Fatihah, you read another short passage from the Qur'an and are allowed to read the same verses you read from the previous Rak'ah. Then, you bow down in Ruku' and just repeat all the previous steps. The only difference comes after your second Sajdah.

#10: Al Tashahhud

Remember, we are now praying Fajr, which consists of two Rak'ah. And since you've done your second Sajdah, you are at the end of the prayer. The final step after your second Sajdah in your second Rak'ah is to sit back in Juluus position, just like you do between the two Sajdatayn (dual plural of Sajdah). Your feet are in the same position, and your palms are on your thighs. This time, you raise the index finger of your right hand.

And you say the following:

"At Tahiyyaatu lilaahi was Salawaatu wat tayibaatu

Assalaamu 'alaika ayyuhan nabiyyu wa rahmatu Allahi wa barakaatuh

Assalaamu 'alaynaa wa 'alaa 'ebaadillaahis saaliheen,

Ash hadu allaa ilaha illa Allah Wa ash hadu anna Muhammadan 'abduhuu wa rasuuluh,"

Then, you say:

"Allahumma salli 'ala Muhammadin wa 'ala aali Muhammad

Kamaa salayta 'ala Ibraaheem wa 'ala aali Ibrahim

Innaka Hameedun Majeed

Wa baarik 'ala Muhammadin wa 'ala aali Muhammad

Kamaa baarakta 'ala Ibraaheem wa 'ala aali Ibrahim

Innaka Hameedun Majeed"

This is the respective translation of both halves:

"All compliments, prayers, and pure words are due to Allah.

Peace be upon you, O Prophet, and the mercy of Allah and His blessings.

Peace be upon us, and on the righteous slaves of Allah.

I bear witness that none has the right to be worshipped except Allah, and I bear witness that Muhammad is His slave and Messenger"

"O Allah, send prayers upon Muhammad and upon the family (or followers) of Muhammad, Just as You sent prayers upon Ibrahim and the family (or followers) of Ibrahim,

Verily, you are full of Praise and Majesty.

O Allah, bless Muhammad and the family (or followers) of Muhammad as You blessed Ibrahim and the family (or followers) of Ibraaheem,

Verily, you are full of Praise and Majesty."

As this is Fajr prayer, you will be saying both the first and the second halves. After that, you look to your right and say: "Assalamu alaykum wa rahmatu Allah," and look to your left and say the same. This is called Tasleem, and it marks the end of your Salah. Congratulations! Now you have prayed, Fajr.

May Allah guide you and us to good and honest deeds.

Dhuhr

Dhuhr is the second prayer of the day, consisting of four Rak'ah. It is prayed at noon.

Note: The gap between Fajr and Dhuhr is the largest gap between two consecutive prayers throughout one day, sitting between about eight and nine hours in most countries. Now let's see how you pray, Dhuhr.

#1: The First Two Rak'atayn

The first two Rak'atayn (dual plural of Rak'ah in Arabic) of Dhuhr are similar to Fajr. You start with intention, of course, and after you say Takbirat al-Ihram, you can recite Dua' al-Thana': *"Subhaanaka Allaahumma wa bihamdika, watabarakasmuka, wa ta'aalaa jadduka, wa laa 'ilaaha ghayruka."*

Here it is in English: "All Glory be to You, O Allah! And Praise Be To You and Blessed Is Your Name and Exalted is Your Majesty and None has the Right to Be Worshiped Besides You."

Then, after Ta'awwudh: *"A'uthu billahi minash shaitanir rajeem,"* you recite Surah al-Fatihah and then a short passage from the Holy Qur'an. In Dhuhr, unlike Fajr, it is better to recite Surah al-Fatihah and a passage from the Holy Qur'an silently. You could simply recite them in a very low voice. From then on, you repeat the same steps as Fajr in the first two Rak'atayn. As we've explained, you should *"Allahu Akbar"* as you are going from each position to the next, except when you are going from Ruku' back to Qiyam, this is the only time you don't say "Allahu Akbar." Instead, you say *"Sami'Allahu liman hamidah."*

#2: The First Tashahhud

This step might make you wonder why it is called the 'first' Tashahhud? Well, in Fajr, since there are only two Rak'atayn, you only say Tashahhud once, and you say both of its halves. Dhuhr, however, consists of four Rak'ah So, after you get up from your second Sujud in the second Rak'ah of Dhuhr, you sit up in Juluus as usual, and you say only the first half of Tashahhud:

"At Tahiyyaatu lilaahi was Salawaatu wat tayibaatu

Assalaamu 'alaika ayyuhan nabiyyu wa rahmatu Allahi wa barakaatuh

Assalaamu 'alaynaa wa 'alaa 'ebaadillaahis saaliheen,

Ash hadu allaa ilaha illa Allah Wa ash hadu anna Muhammadan 'abduhuu wa rasuuluh,"

After that, you get back up to your feet, stand straight, and fold your hands over your chest. Remember to say "Allahu Akbar" as you are getting back up. Now you have finished half of Dhuhr, and you are starting your third Rak'ah.

#3: The Third Rak'ah

In the third Rak'ah, you start as usual. You say, *"Bismillahir Rahmanir Raheem,"* and you recite Surah al-Fatihah. Here is what's different in the third Rak'ah. You don't read a short passage from the Qur'an following Surah al-Fatihah. Remember, this is all still silent recitation, as this is Dhuhr. So, after you recite Surah al-Fatihah, you go straight to Ruku' and *say "Allahu Akbar"* as you go down. After that, you do Ruku' normally by saying: *"Subhana Rabiyal Adhim"* three times, then you get back up as you say *"Sami'Allahu liman hamidah."* Then after saying "Rabanna wa lakal hamd," you go down to Sujud while saying "Allahu Akbar" on the way down to your hands; remember to put your hands first as instructed by the Prophet (PBUH).

In Sujud, as usual, you say *"Subhana Rabiyal A'la"* three times, and you sit up to Juluus, don't forget the Takbir when you're transitioning from one move to another. During Juluus, you say "Rabigh-fir lee" three times, and then you go back down to your second Sujud.

#4: The Fourth Rak'ah

When you finish your second Sujud of your third Rak'ah, you get back up to Qiyam. Now, you've completed your third Rak'ah. It's time for your fourth and final Rak'ah of Salah al-Dhuhr. It is very similar to the third Rak'ah. You start by silently reciting Surah al-Fatihah in the Qiyam position, and you don't follow it with a passage from the Holy Qur'an, a short chapter, or anything. You simply go down straight to Ruku'.

As you've probably noticed, the steps starting from Ruku' are almost the same in all Rak'ah. So, after you get back up from Ruku', you go down to your first Sajdah, sit up in Juluus, and then go back down to your second Sajdah. During Ruku', you say: *"Subhana Rabiyal Adhim"* three times as usual. And when you get up from Ruku', after saying: *"Sami'Allahu liman hamidah,"* you say: *"Rabanna wa lakal hamd."* In Sujud, you say *"Subhana Rabiyal A'la"* three times, and between the two Sajdatayn, you say: *"Rabbigh-fer lee"* three times. Everything is like the previous Rak'ah. Again, don't forget to say *"Allahu Akbar"* when you are going from each position to the next, except when you are coming up from Ruku', say *"Sami'Allahu liman hamidah."* We will explain this briefly Insha'Allah.

After your second Sajdah of your fourth Rak'ah, now your Salah is coming to a close. This is the final step: You sit up in the Juluus position with your palms on your thighs and the right index finger raised. Then, you say the full Tashahhud - both halves:

"At Tahiyyaatu lilaahi was Salawaatu wat tayibaatu

Assalaamu 'alaika ayyuhan nabiyyu wa rahmatu Allahi wa barakaatuh

Assalaamu 'alaynaa wa 'alaa 'ebaadillaahis saaliheen,

Ash hadu allaa ilaha illa Allah Wa ash hadu anna Muhammadan 'abduhuu wa rasuuluh,"

Then, you say:

"Allahumma salli 'ala Muhammadin wa 'ala aali Muhammad

Kamaa salayta 'ala Ibraaheem wa 'ala aali Ibrahim

Innaka Hameedun Majeed

Wa baarik 'ala Muhammadin wa 'ala aali Muhammad

Kamaa baarakta 'ala Ibraaheem wa 'ala aali Ibrahim

Innaka Hameedun Majeed"

After that, you do Tasleem. You look to your right shoulder and say: *"Assalamu alaykum wa rahmatu Allah,"* then you look to your left shoulder and say the same again.

Congratulations again! Now, you have officially prayed, Dhuhr. May Allah (SWT) accept our prayers and guide you and us to more good and honest deeds.

Asr

Asr is the third prayer of the day. It consists of four Rak'aha, just like Dhuhr, and it is prayed in the same way. So, when you hear the Adhan (the call to prayer) for Asr, you pray in the same way as Dhuhr prayer. Remember the intention before anything, as the Prophet (PBUH) has said: "Deeds are but with intentions." We pray Asr in the afternoon when an object's shadow is exactly as long as it is.

Transitional Takbir

We have stressed multiple times before during the previous explanations on saying *"Allahu Akbar"* when you are going from one position to the next except for when you are coming back up from Ruku', for which you say: *"Sami'Allahu liman hamidah."* The action of saying *"Allahu Akbar"* is called Takbir, so the times you are saying *"Allahu Akbar"* between your moves is called Takbirat intiqaliyah, which literally means "Transitional Takbirs." Some schools of Fiqh, which is the study of Islamic jurisprudence, the applications of Shariaah, and a few more concepts in Islamic sciences, argue that Transitional Takbir must take up the entire time you are transitioning between positions exactly during that time. However, it is also okay to just say it as you transition between moves. You don't have to stress about starting to say it exactly as you begin moving from your current position and finishing it exactly as you stop moving and rest in your following position.

Abu Hurairah (May Allah be pleased with him) reported that the Prophet (PBUH) said: "The religion (of Islam) is easy, and whoever makes the religion a rigor, it will overpower him. So, follow a middle course (in worship); if you can't do this, do something near to it and give glad tidings and seek help (of Allah) at morning and at dusk and some part of night." This is one of the beauties of Islam, its ease.

Loud and Silent Recitation

We've talked earlier about how recitation should be aloud in Fajr and silent in Dhuhr. In which prayers do we recite loudly? And in which do we recite silently? The answer to this, as always, we take from the Sunnah of the Prophet (PBUH) as Allah (SWT) says in Surah al-Ahzab chapter 33 verse 21: "The Messenger of Allah is an excellent model for those of you who put your hope in God and the Last Day and remember Allah often." So, Prophet Muhammad (PBUH) has said: "Pray as you have seen me pray."

According to this, Salawat performed during the day are silent, and prayers performed during the night are when you recite loudly. This doesn't include special occasions like Salah al-Jumu'ah (the Friday prayer), Salah al-Eid (the prayer of Eid), and others. The five prayers we've mentioned: Fajr, Dhuhr, Asr, Maghrib, and Isha' are called Salah Fard, meaning they are obligatory. Other prayers are not obligatory. Salawat al-Sunnah, extra prayers done by the Prophet Muhammad (PBUH) other than the five Fard, are the most prominent example. Most Sunnah prayers consist of two Rak'atayn and are prayed just like Fajr, only at different times. We will discuss these extra prayers and other special ones in the final chapter of this book Insha'Allah.

Maghrib

Now that you've prayed Fajr, Dhuhr, and Asr Masha 'Allah, we've come to the fourth prayer of the day, Maghrib. Maghrib is one of the only prayers, Fard and otherwise, consisting of three Rak'ah, a generally uncommon number. We pray Maghrib at sundown and recite loudly. Here's how it goes:

#1: The First Two Rak'atayn

You pray the first two Rak'atayn normally as you would in Dhuhr and Asr. You start with intention, and after Takbirat al Ihram, then Dua' al-Thana' and Ta'awwudh. Then, you recite Surah al-Fatihah, aloud this time because this is Maghrib. Also note that the only thing that must be said aloud is the recitation of the Holy Qur'an, preferably Takbirat al Ihram and all Transitional Takbir. When you're saying *"Subhana Rabiyal Adhim"* during Ruku', for example, or *"Subhana Rabiyal A'la"* during Sujud, you don't have to say them out loud. The recitation of the Noble Qur'an is the most important.

#2: The Third Rak'ah

In Maghrib, like Dhuhr and Asr, you only say the first of Tashahhud after your second Sajdah in your second Rak'ah, and then you get up. In the third Rak'ah, you recite Surah al-Fatihah only. However, you recite it silently. Maghrib is a prayer in which you are supposed to recite aloud, but in the third Rak'ah, you recite silently. This is for recitation.

After silently reciting Surah al-Fatihah and getting up from your second Juluus in the second Rak'ah, you normally bow down in Ruku' and say *"Subhana Rabiyal Adhim"* three times. You come back up saying *"Sami'Allahu liman hamidah"* and say "Rabanna wa lakal hamd," then you go down to your first Sajdah.

You do your two Sajdatayn normally and then sit up after the second Sajdah. You say the full Tashahhud:

"At Tahiyyaatu lilaahi was Salawaatu wat tayibaatu

Assalaamu 'alaika ayyuhan nabiyyu wa rahmatu Allahi wa barakaatuh

Assalaamu 'alaynaa wa 'alaa 'ebaadillaahis saaliheen,

Ash hadu allaa ilaha illa Allah Wa ash hadu anna Muhammadan 'abduhuu wa rasuuluh,"

After that, the second half:

"*Allahumma salli 'ala Muhammadin wa 'ala aali Muhammad*

Kamaa salayta 'ala Ibraaheem wa 'ala aali Ibrahim

Innaka Hameedun Majeed

Wa baarik 'ala Muhammadin wa 'ala aali Muhammad

Kamaa baarakta 'ala Ibraaheem wa 'ala aali Ibrahim

Innaka Hameedun Majeed"

Then, you do Tasleem. You look to your right shoulder and say: "*Assalamu alaykum wa rahmatu Allah,*" then look to your left shoulder and say it again. This is how we pray, Maghrib.

May Allah (SWT) bless you and us with Jannah and guidance to the Right Path (the true path of Islam).

Isha'

After praying Maghrib, we have only one more Fard i.e., Isha'. Isha' is prayed when the night falls completely or when the white twilight is over. This is a little over an hour after Maghrib. So, when you hear the Adhan for Isha', here is what you do.

#1: The First Two Rak'atayn

As we hope you've gotten used to, the first two Rak'atayn are the same. After the true intention of praying to Allah (SWT), and after Takbirat al-Ihram, Dua' al-Thana', and Ta'awwudh, you recite Surah al-Fatihah and a passage from a Qur'an of your choice. Again, length is not an issue; read however long a passage suits you. In Isha', you recite loudly and say the first half of the Tashahhud after your second Sajdah of the second Rak'ah:

"At Tahiyyaatu lilaahi was Salawaatu wat tayibaatu

Assalaamu 'alaika ayyuhan nabiyyu wa rahmatu Allahi wa barakaatuh

Assalaamu 'alaynaa wa 'alaa 'ebaadillaahis saaliheen,

Ash hadu allaa ilaha illa Allah Wa ash hadu anna Muhammadan 'abduhuu wa rasuuluh,"

#2: The Second Two Rak'atayn

After you get up from your second Juluus in the second Rak'ah, you start reciting Surah al-Fatihah again. This is your third Rak'ah. As you did in Maghrib, you recite loudly only for the first two Rak'atayn, while in the third Rak'ah, you recite only Surah al-Fatihah silently. The fourth Rak'ah in Isha' is the same as well.

During the third Rak'ah, after your second Sajdah, you get up to the Qiyam position for the last time to start your fourth Rak'ah. Don't forget Transitional Takbir, of course. After you recite Surah al-Fatihah, bow down in Ruku' and say: *"Subhana Rabiyal Adhim"* three times. After that, get back up and say: *"Sami'Allahu liman hamidah,"* as you get up. Then, say: *"Rabanna wa lakal hamd"* and go down to Sujud.

Remember, in Sujud, your toes, knees, hands, forehead, and nose must all touch the ground. You say: *"Subhana Rabiyal A'la"* three times. This is your first Sajdah of the fourth Rak'ah. After this Sajdah, you sit up in the Juluus position and do Sujud one more time. Then, you sit up in Juluus one last time and say the full Tashahhud:

"At Tahiyyaatu lilaahi was Salawaatu wat tayibaatu

Assalaamu 'alaika ayyuhan nabiyyu wa rahmatu Allahi wa barakaatuh

Assalaamu 'alaynaa wa 'alaa 'ebaadillaahis saaliheen,

Ash hadu allaa ilaha illa Allah Wa ash hadu anna Muhammadan 'abduhuu wa rasuuluh,"

After that, the second half:

"Allahumma salli 'ala Muhammadin wa 'ala aali Muhammad

Kamaa salayta 'ala Ibraaheem wa 'ala aali Ibrahim

Innaka Hameedun Majeed

Wa baarik 'ala Muhammadin wa 'ala aali Muhammad

Kamaa baarakta 'ala Ibraaheem wa 'ala aali Ibrahim

Innaka Hameedun Majeed"

After that, you do Tasleem, and Congratulations!! You have prayed the five Fard prayers. May Allah (SWT) accept your and our good deeds and make our intentions pure.

Salah in the Mosque

Allah (SWT) says in Surah al-Baqarah chapter 2, verse 114: "And who is more unjust than he who prevents (praying in) the mosques of Allah so that His name be not mentioned in them, and endeavors (diligently) for their ruin? Those can in no way enter them except in fear, for them is disgrace in the present life, and in the Hereafter, they will have a tremendous torment." This calls us to stress on praying in mosques. The mosques of Allah are houses of worship and are meant to be prayed in. This, however, is for men only. Men are the only ones 'obliged' to pray in mosques. By obligation, we don't mean that it's ordained, but simply that it is only asked of men. Women are better advised to pray at home for their own protection, while men are encouraged to pray in mosques. Thus, we encourage you and ourselves to pray as much of the Fara'id (plural of Fard) prayers in mosques.

Manners in the Mosque

Now that we've said you should pray in a mosque. How should you? There are, of course, manners for praying and being in a mosque. First of all, take off your shoes before you go in. You will most likely find shelves to put your shoes on near the door Insha'Allah. Secondly, be careful not to make any noise as this may distract other people who are praying or may disturb others. Thirdly, you should pray two Rak'atayn. These are called Tahiyat al-Masjid (lit. the Salute of the Mosque). These are non-obligatory but preferable. These are prayed exactly like Fajr, although silently.

Now, onto the Fard prayers. When you are praying with a group of people, it is called Salah Jama'ah (lit. a group prayer). Prophet Muhammad (PBUH) has been reported to say: "Praying in congregation is twenty-five times better than praying alone." Another report says: "Twenty-seven." Despite the difference in numbers, both emphasize the virtue of Salah al-Jama'ah over performing Salah alone. The one leading the prayers is called the Imam; this is a great honor and is not earned easily. May Allah make you and us good examples to those aware of Him.

What's easier about Salah Jama'ah is that all you have to do is follow the Imam's movements. There are some differences between praying behind an Imam and praying alone.

While praying Salah alone, you are supposed to recite some parts loudly. However, when you are praying behind an Iman, it is only he who recites loudly. After the Imam finishes reciting Surah al-Fatihah, you must say Ameen, along with your brothers who are praying with you. After that, you listen to him reciting a passage of the Qur'an and follow along with his movements.

In fact, when you are praying behind an Imam in a congregation in a Salah with loud recitation, you do not recite at all. This follows Allah's command (SWT) as He says in Surah al-A'raf chapter 7 verse 204: "And when the Qur'an is read, then listen to it and hearken, that possibly you would be granted mercy." Otherwise, Salah behind an Imam is mostly the same. The Imam recites silently during Salah with silent recitation, and so do you. Just remember never to fall behind. And this is in Salah al-Jama'ah only. If you haven't finished reciting Surah al-Fatihah and the Imam says "Allahu Akbar" to go down to Ruku, you stop reciting, and you go with him. An Imam should normally be considerate in his pace of the people praying behind him but know this just in case.

Chapter 4: Common Mistakes in Salah

We've learned Alhamdulillah about Salah and how to perform it. However, there are some common mistakes that we should avoid. Some of these might even make your Salah unacceptable. Let's discuss these mistakes and how to avoid them.

Lack of Concentration

Allah (SWT) says in Surat al-Mu'minoon chapter 23, verses 1 and 2: "Successful indeed are the believers. Those who offer their Salah with all solemnity and full submissiveness." This is the meaning of Khushu'. Lack of concentration lies in a few things. Firstly, some people, may Allah guide us and them to the Right Path, look to their sides while praying if something catches their eye. This is fine if done by mistake but isn't if done on purpose. Some people, especially when they are among people who have been praying for many years, don't pay attention to the words they're saying because their minds are distracted or because Shaytan comes to them. You can avoid this by doing a few simple things. First of all, say

Ta'awwudh: *"A'uthu billahi minash shaitanir rajeem"* before starting your Salah and making Niyyah. Secondly, remember the Greatness of Allah (SWT) and the importance of standing in front of your Mighty Creator. Thirdly, you should choose a place without distractions and disturbance. Mosques are the best option for men, if available. However, a quiet room at home is the best option for women. For people who work under a manager, asking your manager for a quiet room to pray in is the best practice. Don't forget your intention before Salah, of course.

6. *A lack of concentration during prayer should be avoided at all costs.*
Source: https://www.pexels.com/photo/woman-in-black-hijab-sitting-beside-woman-in-black-hijab-7249338/

Mispronunciation and Errors in Recitation

This issue is very controversial because it is a lot more common than initially perceived. A few mispronunciations by non-Arabic speakers are tolerable, but disregarding Tashkeel (Arabic diacritics) and sometimes the unwell memorization of the Holy Qur'an is malpractice. You must memorize Surah al-Fatihah well, as this is the one Surah that you read in all Salawat. After that, start by memorizing short Surahs of the Qur'an. Juz' 30 is a great place to start because it has the shortest chapters of the Holy Qur'an. If your first language isn't Arabic, you should ask Allah (SWT) for guidance and try to learn Arabic to the best of your abilities, as this can improve your recitation and understanding of the Holy Qur'an.

Mistakes, because they are unintentional by definition, don't invalidate your Salah. It's just important to be wary of them as avoiding them gets you closer to perfecting your Salah. Also, know that if you're praying behind an Imam with loud recitation and you hear them make a mistake, you are to correct them. You do that by simply saying the correct word he missed out loud; he should correct himself and reread the part he read wrong the first time. This is one of the simplest mistakes to avoid, so don't stress about it and try learning proper pronunciation to please Allah (SWT). May Allah (SWT) bless you and us with his Infinite Mercy.

Rushing through Salah

This is one of the most common mistakes among many Muslims, may Allah (SWT) guide them and us to His Right Path. Allah (SWT) says in Surah al-Muzammil chapter 73 verse 4: "And recite the Qur'an (aloud) in a slow, (pleasant tone and) style." Take your time with Salah. You stand praying to the Creator of the Universe; mind your situation well. You don't have to prolong Salah, but absolutely do not rush it. Rushing is an issue because of many things. Firstly, it doesn't show your respect to the Salah and to the fact you're standing before Allah (SWT). Secondly, it generates more mistakes. You might not pay proper attention to your recitation and your words, and you might miss something.

Recite the Qur'an carefully and ponder the meanings of Allah's Holy Word (SWT). Give Salah its justice. Pronounce every word to its fullest. Say: "Subhana Rabiyal Adhim" and "Subhana Rabiyal A'la" without speeding through them. You must achieve calmness and tranquility in your Salah. Breathe with every movement, and remember you stand before Allah Almighty. Nothing could be more important. Don't worry about anything around you. Don't worry about returning to your desk, as this might be common with people who have to pray while working. Remember that rushing Salah is also an attribute of Munafiqin (Hypocrites), so please be careful.

Incomplete or Incorrect Performance

This mistake happens quite often, although not as common as the ones mentioned above. First of all, any willful violation of any Wajib act in Salah invalidates that. Wajib acts are compulsory ones, so reciting Surah al-Fatihah, for example, is a Wajib. Takbirat al-Ihram is a Wajib act, so are Sujud and Ruku'. Wajib acts define Salah, so any violation of them can invalidate your Salah.

On the other hand, one might simply forget something; we are only human, after all. A common mistake is forgetting to sit up for the first Tashahhud in the second Rak'ah of Salawat with four Rak'ah: Dhuhr, Asr, and Isha'. One could simply get up quickly. If this is an honest mistake, then it's fine. Remember that Allah (SWT) is the Most Merciful and that His religion is one of ease.

Let's look at a situation where you unintentionally miss an action or position. Let's say you are praying, Asr, and you are in your first Rak'ah. You are doing your first Sajdah, and after saying *"Subhana Rabiyal A'la"* three times, you get up right away. Then, later on in your Salah, you remember that you missed your second Sajdah in the first Rak'ah. You continue praying normally until your last Rak'ah; after your second Sajdah, you say the full Tashahhud normally, but then you don't do Taslim immediately. You bow down in Sujud, say: *"Subhana Rabiyal Adhim"* three times, and sit back in Juluus. In this Juluus, you say: "Rabbigh-fer lee" three times, as usual, and you go back down for one more Sajdah, and you say: "Subhana Rabiyal Adhim" three times again. After that, you get up and do Tasleem immediately, ending your Salah. The two Sajdatayn you just did are called Sajdatayn Sahw; Sahw translates to inattention or oversight. This way, your Salah is valid. But remember, it must be an honest mistake, you can't miss a move on purpose thinking you're just going to do two Sajdatayn Sahw, and that's it. Sajdatayn Sahw is for when you truly forget. This way, you've learned about some of the most common mistakes in Salah. Make sure to avoid them, may Allah (SWT) bless you and us with his Infinite Mercy.

Chapter 5: Enhancing the Quality of Salah

We've talked about the common mistakes made during Salah and how to avoid them. Now, how do we make our Salah better in order to please Allah (SWT) more? How do we get closer to our Creator with our Salah?

Khushu'

Khushu' is one of the most important aspects of your Salah. In simple terms, Khushu' is focusing on your Salah and only that. Remember, you stand before the Almighty Rahman and act accordingly. It is reported that 'Abdullah ibn Abbas, one of the companions of the Prophet (PBUH), said: "Two Rak'ah with contemplation are better than standing for the entire night with an inattentive heart." Salah is not a charade or a sequence of movements. It is time you take out of your day to obey Allah (SWT) and connect with Him. To try and attain this, it is important to be calm and don't rush your Salah. Servitude to Allah (SWT) has its sweetness; savor it. Vary the Surahs you read after Surah al-Fatihah; this helps you stay more focused. This also pushes you to memorize more of the

Holy Qur'an, so it's a win on two fronts. Last but not least, understand what you are saying. Allah (SWT) urges Muslims to ponder his Holy Book, so do that, and you shall Insha'Allah find in it beauty and the Infinite Wisdom of Allah (SWT). May I remind you that Allah (SWT) says in Surah al-A'raf chapter 7, verse 204: "And when the Qur'an is read, then listen to it and hearken, that possibly you would be granted mercy."

Beautifying Recitation

Prophet Muhammad (PBUH) has been reported to say: "Beautify the Qur'an with your voices." And he also said: "He who does not recite the Qur'an melodiously is not one of us." If you've heard any Qari' (lit. reader in Arabic) of the Holy Qur'an, you probably know about this. Try listening to Qura' (plural of Qari') and see how they read. Listen well, imitate them, and live with the Ayah (verses). You must know how different it is to listen to an Ayah recited like that and when you simply read it normally. The difference is vast. Here are some recommendations for skillful Qura' of the Holy Qur'an: the Saudi Abu Bakr Shatri, the Egyptian Abdul Basit Abdul Samad, and the Egyptian Muhammad Al-Minshawi. You don't have to stick to the style of one Qari'; of course, develop your own voice. Learn Tajwid and know how to recite and pronounce it beautifully. You could try reciting the Qur'an daily and listening to Qura' as well. When you make this a habit, you'll find your voice getting better and better sooner or later Insha'Allah. But remember to have patience and work for it, may Allah (SWT) bless you and us with his Infinite Mercy.

7. Beautifying your recitation allows you to focus on the Salah.
Source: https://www.pexels.com/photo/close-up-photo-of-pages-of-the-holy-quran-with-prayer-beads-6920597/

Strengthening Your Spirituality

In earlier chapters, we talked a lot about intention before your actions and your deeds towards Allah (SWT). This serves to remind you, as well, of our main purpose. We do Salah to please Allah (SWT); remember this in all of your actions, not just Salah. When done correctly, this provides a sense of peace and truth you cannot imagine. Allah (SWT) says in Surah Muhammad chapter 47, verse 2: "And the ones who have believed and done deeds of righteousness and have believed in what has been successively sent down upon Muhammad, and it is the Truth from their Lord-He will expiate for them their odious deeds and will make righteous their state."

Before you go into Salah, think about where you're going for a moment. You stand before Allah (SWT), reciting his

Holy Word, contemplating it, and pondering its meanings. In the simple movements of Salah, you connect with Allah (SWT) in a manner unlike any other deed in all of Islam. During Sujud, you do Dua' asking the mercy of Allah (SWT). During Juluus, you ask Him (SWT) for forgiveness. During Ruku' and Sujud, you mention and glorify His name: *"Subhana Rabiyal Adhim," "Subhana Rabiyal A'la."* Think about every one of these movements and what it means in your relationship with Allah (SWT).

Seeking Knowledge and Understanding the Meaning

This part is the most exciting, in a sense. As we've said before, you must ponder the Noble Qur'an and contemplate its Holy Ayah. This is important during Salah and when reading the Qur'an in general. Allah (SWT) says in Surah Sad chapter 38 verse 29: "A Book We have sent down to you, Blessed, that they may ponder over its Ayah (verses, signs) and that men endowed with intellects would remind themselves." Think about the deeper meaning of each verse you recite in your Salah: the Ayah about Jannah, the Ayah with commandments.

A common question in this area is: "How?" Take the Ayah with Jannah, for example. When you recite them in Qiyam and go down to Sujud, ask Allah (SWT) for Jannah in your Dua'. For Ayah, with commandments, think to yourself, "Do I do this? Am I following this correctly?" Try reading Tafsir. This helps tremendously with seeking knowledge and understanding of the Qur'an and shall Insha'Allah, make your Salah better.

We've learned how to enhance our Salah and be closer to Allah (SWT) during our prayers. Earlier, we mentioned that there are Salah that are different from the regular Fard. Let's talk about them in the next chapter.

Chapter 6: Salah in Special Circumstances

The only obligatory Salawat in Islam are the five Fard: Fajr, Dhuhr, Asr, Maghrib, and Isha'. However, other Salawat besides these can bring you closer to Allah (SWT) Insha'Allah if you do them. Let's know them.

Salah al-Jumu'a

8.   *The Friday prayer is usually done in a group at the mosque. Source: https://unsplash.com/photos/Y2oE2uNLSrs*

This literally means the Friday prayer. Salah al-Jumu'a is only a different form of Dhuhr; Dhuhr is prayed differently on Fridays. These are its steps:

#1: Khutbah

Khutba is a sermon given by the Imam of the mosque every Friday right after the Adhan of Dhuhr. It is obligatory for men to attend it at the mosque, for men who can, so young children below the age of puberty are exempted from the obligation, and so are elders incapable of going out. This sermon focuses on a certain topic, mostly something contemporary. The news of the Muslim Ummah (lit. nation in Arabic) is a popular topic. A Khutbah could be about a Hadith of the Prophet Muhammad (PBUH) or an Ayah of the Holy Qur'an. The topic is up to the Imam, giving the Khutbah to choose, but you are to listen intently. May Allah (SWT) grant us His infinite mercy.

#2: Two Rak'atayn

This is the major difference in Dhuhr of Friday. After hearing the Khutbah, you pray two Rak'atayn behind the Imam. These two Rak'atayn, however, are with loud recitation. Since you are praying behind an Imam, you are to listen and say *"Ameen"* when he finishes Surah al-Fatihah. Don't forget your intention before you start your Salah.

After Surah al-Fatihah and the short passage of the Qur'an, you do Ruku' normally, followed by Qiyam again. After that you do Sujud and so on. In the second Sajdah of the second Rak'ah, you say the full Tashahhud:

"At Tahiyyaatu lilaahi was Salawaatu wat tayibaatu

Assalaamu 'alaika ayyuhan nabiyyu wa rahmatu Allahi wa barakaatuh

Assalaamu 'alaynaa wa 'alaa 'ebaadillaahis saaliheen,

Ash hadu allaa ilaha illa Allah Wa ash hadu anna Muhammadan 'abduhuu wa rasuuluh,"

After that, the second half:

"Allahumma salli 'ala Muhammadin wa 'ala aali Muhammad

Kamaa salayta 'ala Ibraaheem wa 'ala aali Ibrahim

Innaka Hameedun Majeed

Wa baarik 'ala Muhammadin wa 'ala aali Muhammad

Kamaa baarakta 'ala Ibraaheem wa 'ala aali Ibrahim

Innaka Hameedun Majeed"

You follow that by Tasleem: "Assalamu 'alaykum wa Rahmat Ullah" to your right shoulder once and then to your left shoulder. This is how you pray, Salah al-Jumu'a. For people who don't pray Jumu'a at the mosque, they just pray Dhuhr normally. Please consider well your excuse for not attending, as the Khutbah is part of the Fard.

Salah al-Musafir

This means the Traveler's prayer. Often during travel, people are tired, especially if their traveling takes numerous hours, but Allah (SWT) has given His religion, Islam, the attribute of ease, so when you are traveling, Salah is a little shorter.

Dhuhr and Asr

Dhuhr and Asr are shortened to two Rak'atayn each instead of four. You are allowed to join them and pray both at the time of Dhuhr. So, when you hear the Adhan of Dhuhr, you pray two Rak'atayn silently, and that's Dhuhr. Then, right after Tasleem from these two Rak'atayn, you get up to pray two more Rak'atayn; these are for Asr. This way, when you hear Asr, you don't pray it again. This is, of course, supposing you are traveling at that exact time. You should only do this joining, known as Jam' (lit. joining in Arabic) when it is too difficult to pray the two prayers apart.

Maghrib and Isha'

Maghrib and Isha' are also shortened to two Rak'atayn each but are both prayed in the time of Isha,' the later one's time instead of the earlier one. So, when you hear the Adhan for Isha', you pray two Rak'atayn. That's Maghrib. Then, two more. That is Isha'. Again, Jam' is only advised when it is too difficult to pray the prayers apart.

Fajr

As Fajr is already two Rak'atayn, you can't shorten it further, and you have to pray it on time.

Keep in mind that this is a license given by Allah (SWT). Your Salah is shorter in length but as complete a deed as a normal Salah. Prophet Muhammad (PBUH) has been reported to say: "Allah (SWT) loves that His permissions be practiced, just as he dislikes that disobedience to Him be committed." Allah (SWT) has given you this permission, so use it as He is pleased to make servitude easier for Muslims.

A traveler is granted this permission if his traveling distance is 50 miles or more, which is about 80 kilometers. If you don't intend to stay at the place you've traveled to, you intend to leave as soon as your business is finished; you are allowed Qasr (shortening Salah) until you leave the place you've traveled to. If you intend to stay for more than four days, you are to perform the full Salawat.

Salah al-Janazah

Janazah literally means funeral in Arabic. Funeral prayers include no Ruku' and no Sujud and are always prayed silently regardless of the time of the day. They consist of four Takbirat (plural of one Takbirah, which is when you say "Allahu Akbar").

#1: Takbirat al-Ihram

You stand up in Qiyam and you say "Allahu Akbar", raising your hands to the sides of your ears. After that all you do is recite Surah al-Fatihah:

"Al hamdu lil lahi rabbil 'alamin. Arrahmanir rahim. Maliki yawmiddin. Iyyaka na'budu wa iyyaka nasta'in. Ihdinas siratal mustaqim. Siratal ladhina an'amta'alaihim, ghairil maghdubi'alaihim wa lad dhallin. (Ameen)"

#2: The Second Takbirah

After Surah al-Fatihah, you say *"Allahu Akbar"* once more while still standing up in Qiyam position. You don't go down to do Ruku'. After this Takbirah, you say the second half of the Tashahhud:

"Allahumma salli 'ala Muhammadin wa 'ala aali Muhammad

Kamaa salayta 'ala Ibraaheem wa 'ala aali Ibrahim

Innaka Hameedun Majeed

Wa baarik 'ala Muhammadin wa 'ala aali Muhammad

Kamaa baarakta 'ala Ibraaheem wa 'ala aali Ibrahim

Innaka Hameedun Majeed"

#3: The Third Takbirah

After that, you say "Allahu Akbar" one more time. Now, you do Dua' for the deceased, asking Allah (SWT) Jannah and Mercy for them. A good Dua' is:

"Allahuma igh-fir lahu wa irhamh birahmatika ya Arham ar-Rahimeen" if it's a male, and *"Allahuma igh-fir laha wa irhamha birahmatika ya Arham ar-Rahimeen"* if it's a female.

The former means: "O Allah, the Most Merciful of the merciful, forgive him and bless him with Your Mercy," and the latter means: "O Allah, the Most Merciful of the merciful, forgive her and bless her with Your Mercy."

#4: The Fourth Takbirah

After that, you say *"Allahu Akbar"* one last time and do Dua' for yourself and all Muslims. You could say: *"Allahuma igh-fir lana wa irhamna birahmatika ya Arham ar-Rahimeen,"* which means: "O Allah, the Most Merciful of the merciful, forgive us and bless us with Your Mercy."

After that, you do Tasleem. You look to your right shoulder, remember you are still standing up, and say: *"Assalamu 'alaykum wa Rahmat Ullah,"* then look to your left shoulder and say the same.

If you are praying behind an Imam, which is more likely in Salawat al-Janazah, follow the Takbirat of the Imam. Even if you haven't finished Surah al-Fatihah after the first Takbirah and the Imam does the second Takbirah, do the second Takbirah and start the second half of the Tashahhud and so on. You must raise your hands to the sides of your ears during the first Takbirah, Takbirat al-Ihram, while it is an option in the following Takbirat; you may raise your hands or not, but you have to say *"Allahu Akbar."*

Salah al-Eid

Salah al-Eid is prayed twice a year. The first is on the first day of Eid al-Fitr, on the first day of the month of Shawwal, which comes after Ramadan, and the second is on the first day of Eid al-Adha, on the tenth of the month of Dhul' Hijja. Salah al-Eid consists of only two Rak'atayn and is very simple. It is the same for both Eids. It is prayed in the very early morning, shortly after dawn.

#1: Clothing and Takbirat

First of all, it is of the Sunnah of the Prophet Muhammad (PBUH) to wear nice clothes, especially on the occasion of Eid. Most people buy new clothes for themselves and their loved ones, which is even better. On the day of Eid, you will most likely hear Takbirat al-Eid coming from mosques around you.

"Allahu Akbar, Allahu Akbar, Allahu Akbar, La Ilaha illa Allah

Allahu Akbar, Allahu Akbar wa lillah al-Hamd"

It is Sunnah to do these Takbirat along with the mosque at home, on the street, in your car, or anywhere as long as it is the day of Eid before Salah al-Eid.

#2: Takbirat of the First Rak'ah

What is different about Salah al-Eid is the number of Takbirat. Salah al-Eid has a total of twelve major Takbirat. In the first Rak'ah, you start with Takbirat al-Ihram. *"Allahu*

Akbar," then you say *"Allahu Akbar"* again six more times. That is a total of seven. This is for the first Rak'ah. As this Salah is prayed at the mosque, you must follow the Imam. After that, Surah al-Fatihah comes normally, a short passage, and then Ruku' and Sujud as usual. This Salah has loud recitation, so all you have to do is say *"Ameen"* after the Imam finishes Surah al-Fatihah and listen as he recites the short passage of the Holy Qur'an. Keep in mind that this is still a Salah to Allah (SWT), so focus on the Ayah.

#3: The Second Rak'ah

The second Rak'ah starts with the Transitional Takbir from the Sujud of the first Rak'ah, as usual, and then you add four more Takbirat for a total of five. In both Rak'atayn, you raise your hands to the sides of your ears with every Takbirah.

Taraweeh

Taraweeh prayers are one of the special features of the Sacred Month of Ramadan. Taraweeh prayers are prayed at night, right after Isha', and have loud recitations. They are normally prayed in sets of two Rak'atayn and only in Ramadan. There is no actual constraint on the number of Rak'ah you pray as long as you pray them two at a time. Mosques generally tend to do eight; four sets of two, with a break between the first four and the second four. This break is sometimes only a few minutes long for the Imam and the people praying behind him to rest, and then Salah commences right away once again, and sometimes there is a short Khutbah given by the Imam. This Khutbah is shorter than the Khutbah of Jumu'ah, and the topics are generally more compact.

It is up to you to pray Taraweeh at home or at the mosque. Again, pray for as long as you like. Prophet Muhammad (PBUH) has been reported to say: "Choose such actions as you are capable of performing, for Allah (SWT) does not grow weary. The most beloved religion to Him is that in which a person persists." As long as your intention is the satisfaction of Allah (SWT), do what you can and do not push yourself, for Islam is a religion of ease.

Each two of the Raka'ah you pray in Taraweeh are identical to Fajr, except for the timing. You start with the intention of praying Taraweeh, then you do Takbirat al-Ihram, Dua' al-Thana', Ta'awwudh, and start reciting Surah al-Fatihah and so on until you say the full Tashahhud after the second Sajdah of the second Rak'ah, then you do Tasleem. After that, you get up and pray another two Rak'atayn, and so on. If you go to pray at a mosque and you wish to pray with the Imam for only the first two or four, for example, you are allowed to leave after you achieve the number you desire. Just know that this is a tremendous chance to get closer to Allah (SWT) as the recitation of the Qur'an during Taraweeh is often preferred lengthier, and you get to listen more of the Qur'an and ponder and think more.

Salah During Illness

When we fall ill, Salah is often not easily performed. However, Allah (SWT) has made Islam a religion of ease, and in whatever state you are in, you are allowed to pray. If you can't pray standing up, you can pray sitting. If you can't pray sitting, you can pray lying on your side. May Allah (SWT) protect us and all Muslims from all forms of illness.

#1: Sitting

If you can't stand, sit on a chair in the direction of Qiblah with your back propped up as much as you can and fold your hands over your chest, and your feet should be flat on the floor. This position replaces Qiyam, so in this position, you do Takbirat al-Ihram, recite Dua' al-Thana, and then recite Surah al-Fatihah, and a short passage of the Qur'an.

#2: Ruku' and Sujud while sitting

When you go down for Ruku', bend down simply while you are still sitting and put your hands on the place they're supposed to normally be during Juluus and say: *"Subhana Rabiyal Adhim"* three times, as usual.

When you return from Ruku', sit up while still on the chair. After that, for Sujud, bend down the same way you did when doing Ruku' and say: *"Subhana Rabiyal A'la"* three times. For Juluus, you sit back up and say: *"Rabigh-fer lee"* three times and go down for Sujud again. After this Sajdah, you get back up to your sitting position and start reciting Surah al-Fatihah again for the second Rak'ah. This is how you pray one Rak'ah when you can't stand up. It is permissible to do with any Fard prayer, but you cannot shorten the number of Rak'ah; you have to pray the same number of Rak'ah.With this, we conclude our book. May Allah (SWT) guide you and us to good deeds in the present and the future, and May He forgive us for our sins.

Assalamu 'alaykum wa Rahmatullahi Wa Barakatuh.

Manuscript 2

Why We Pray in Islam

A Guide to Deepening Your Connection to Allah Through Salah and Islamic Prayer

Introduction

Islamic prayer, better known as Salah or Salat, is a fundamental part of the Muslim faith, allowing believers a strong connection with their creator and bringing calm and peace to their lives. This book will give you an important insight into the purpose of prayer, the benefits, and the rituals or practices critical to Islamic prayer. We'll also address a few common misconceptions and answer some of the most asked questions about Salah.

Muslims consider prayer as their time to talk to Allah (SWT), think about their lives, and ask for forgiveness and guidance. Through their prayer, they can cultivate their faith and find solace in what tends to be a chaotic, busy world.

Whether you already follow the Muslim faith and want to understand prayer better or are curious about this aspect of their faith, this guide will give you a comprehensive look at Salah and its importance. This is an easy-to-read guide with step-by-step instructions where needed and an explanation of all the terms mentioned.

Chapter 1: The Concept of Prayer in Islam

Salah is an important act of worship in the Muslim faith. It is also the second of the Five Pillars of Islam, hugely significant and a major part of spiritual practice for all Muslims. Prayer allows them to communicate directly with Allah (God).

The main purpose of praying in Islam is to express gratitude, devotion, and submission to Allah (SWT). It helps Muslims connect deeply with Allah (SWT), seeking His forgiveness, guidance, and blessings. By praying, Muslims can acknowledge that they depend on Allah (SWT) and have complete trust and faith in him.

1. *Prayer is one of the most important concepts in Islam. Source:*
https://unsplash.com/photos/gp_veO5Otmo

Praying in Islam is not as simple as just kneeling and bowing your head. Muslims must follow specific rituals and practices, not to mention physical movements, and recite specific prayers. While these prayers should be recited in Arabic, those who cannot read or write Arabic are still encouraged to pray using their language, but they are, however, expected to learn Arabic gradually.

There are ritual actions a Muslim must take during Salah, which include cleansing and specific ways to stand, bow, sit, and prostrate themselves before Allah (SWT). Later, we'll talk about the significance of the five obligatory daily prayers, each of which should be observed at specific times. For now, they are:

- **Fajr** – Starts as dawn breaks and ends just before sunrise

- **Dhuhr** – Starts just after midday

- **Asr** – Between late afternoon and must be finished before sunset

- **Maghrib** – Starts right after sunset

- **Isha** – Starts once twilight is gone

On top of these, congregational prayers are held every Friday in mosques and at the two festivals that take place yearly:

- **Eid ul-Adha** follows the last day of the Hajj pilgrimage and lasts 3 days.

- **Eid ul-Fitr** is a 3-day festival that starts when Ramadan ends.

Prayer is not just a mechanical act of words and movements; it also has plenty of spiritual and mental benefits. It is a time for Muslims to reflect, show humility, and rejuvenate themselves spiritually. Muslims use this time to focus their hearts and times on Allah (SWT), blocking everything else out.

To sum up, prayer in Islam is an important part of Muslim life, a way to worship Allah (SWT), forge a spiritual connection with him, and bring about personal transformation. It also helps Muslims keep Allah (SWT) in their minds and brings a sense of righteousness, inner peace, and spiritual fulfillment.

A Brief History of Prayer in Islam

Islamic prayer dates back to the 7th century and the Prophet Muhammad (PBUH). The Angel Gabriel revealed the concept and practice of prayer to the Prophet Muhammed

(PBUH), making it clear that the Islamic faith revolved around it. When he received his first revelations from Allah (SWT), the Prophet Muhammed (PBUH) secluded himself and started praying and seeking reflection and solitude.

That first form of Islamic prayer was called the Standing Prayer, or Salat-al-Qiyam. As more people began to follow the Muslim faith, a new form of practice emerged, congregational prayer, with the Prophet Muhammed (PBUH) leading the Muslim community in their prayer practice.

Initially, they prayed toward Jerusalem because all previous Abrahamic faiths had prayed in the same direction. However, by the command of Allah (SWT), this was later changed to the Kaaba in Mecca. This was the act that indicated that the Islamic faith was uniquely significant.

The Prophet Muhammed (PBUH) set the example that dictated the structure and rituals of their prayers, which were established gradually. He formalized the prayers by introducing movements and prostrations and also added specific Qur'an verses, which must be recited; the verses depend on the prayer.

During the Prophet Muhammed's (PBUH) life, the importance of prayer was highlighted, and Muslims were told to establish and maintain a regular prayer schedule. Thus, the five daily prayers came about, and the specific times they must be recited were unveiled. The Prophet Muhammed (PBUH) led the community, teaching them how to perform the prayers correctly.

The Prophet Muhammed (PBUH) died in June 632 AD, but the Muslim community continued their prayer practice. The Sahaba (the Prophet's companions) had an important role to play in preserving the prayer rituals and teachings, and they were responsible for spreading the word throughout all Islamic lands. Those narrations and practices are now an important source for all Muslims.

Islamic scholars learned more about prayer by interpreting the Prophet Muhammed's (PBUH) sayings and actions as time passed. They examined the law, or fiqh of prayer, and examined prayer times, actions, conditions, and spirituality. As a result, different schools began to emerge, each having their own prayer practices and interpretations. These schools provided followers with a guide and rulings on how prayer should be performed.

Throughout the history of Islam, prayer has been one of the pillars of faith, unchanging and central to the Muslim faith. Muslims have practiced it all over the world, in different cultures and regions, since the early Islamic empires and continue to do so today. Their places of worship are the Mosques, where they come together as a community to worship.

The Five Pillars of Islam

These are central to Islam and are the five acts of worship. Think of them as the building blocks to help Muslims in their spiritual journey:

1. **Shahada** – This is the first pillar, the declaration of faith, which requires Muslims to bear witness and proclaim their belief that *"there is no god but Allah, and Muhammed is His messenger."* The declaration in Arabic is:

   La ilaha illa Allah,

   Muhammadun rasul Allah.

This is the core of every Muslim's faith in Islam.

2. **Salah** – The second pillar is prayer, specifically the five daily obligatory prayers. Every Muslim is obligated to pray at certain times of the day, and they must learn specific verses from the Qur'an for each one, physical movements, and supplications. All this is done facing the Kaaba in Mecca.

3. **Zakat** – The third pillar is charity, the giving of alms to those less fortunate. If Muslims meet certain wealth criteria, they are obligated to give 2.5 % of their yearly savings to help poor people and those in need. This purifies their wealth and brings about compassion and social solidarity.

4. **Sawm** – This is the fourth pillar, and it is about fasting. Muslims are obligated to observe Ramadan. This falls in the Islamic Lunar calendar's 9th month, and fasting lasts for the entire month. It doesn't mean they cannot eat anything for the whole month, though they must abstain from physical needs, eating, and drinking from dawn to dusk every day during the month. It is considered a way of building self-discipline, empathy towards the hungry, and spiritual reflection.

5. **Hajj** – The fifth pillar is the pilgrimage. Muslims should head to Mecca in Saudi Arabia at least one time in their life. However, this is not obligatory and depends on an individual's financial condition and physical health. It occurs during Dhul-Hijjah, the Islamic calendar's twelfth and most sacred month. Muslims must perform certain rituals in Mecca and around it; this includes standing on the Arafat plain, walking around the Kaaba, and stoning the devil –

symbolically, of course. The pilgrimage involves a large number of Muslims from around the world gathering together as a symbol of equality, unity, and submission to Allah (SWT).

These five pillars provide the foundations for every Muslim's life. They are not considered obligations; they are acts of worship that strengthen the ties between them and Allah (SWT), promoting compassion, kindness, and social harmony.

Chapter 2: The Significance of Prayer

Prayer is important to any Muslim's life because it guides their actions, thoughts, and spiritual growth. It is a means of seeking blessings and guidance from Allah (SWT) of worship and spiritual connection. Muslims try to align their lives with Islamic principles and teachings, developing deep devotion and faith when they pray.

There are plenty of benefits to prayer, and I've split them into 3 sections for ease of reading.

2. *There are various benefits to performing prayers in Islam. Source: https://unsplash.com/photos/d5Nk3q23ky4*

Spiritual Benefits

Praying in Islam brings several spiritual benefits, including the most important ones listed below:

- **A Deeper Connection with Allah (SWT):** Prayer provides Muslims with a means to connect deeply with Allah (SWT), allowing them to talk intimately with their Creator and seek forgiveness, guidance, and blessings. This connection makes them feel closer to Allah (SWT) and gives them a stronger understanding of His presence in their lives.

- **Spiritual Nourishment:** Prayer is also considered a way of increasing spirituality. It allows Muslims a time for reflection, peace, and tranquility, away from the distractions and challenges of life. This is the time when they can find comfort and solace and allow their souls to rejuvenate.

- **Spiritual Purification:** Muslims consider prayer a way to purify their hearts and souls. When they participate in regular prayer, they can ask for forgiveness, repent for any sins, and work toward improving themselves. Prayer is a reminder that they must align their intentions and actions with Islamic teachings, which results in spiritual transformation and growth.

- **Better Presence of Mind:** During prayer, Muslims must focus their hearts and minds only on Allah (SWT). This mindfulness practice helps them develop attention spans and concentration and gives them a better awareness of their relationship with Allah (SWT). It encourages Muslims to be fully present in the moment, detached from everything else in the world, and connect with the Divine presence.

- **Spiritual Discipline:** Prayer gives a Muslim a real sense of regularity and discipline. Because they must observe set times for their prayers and perform their rituals with consistency and devotion, it instills a commitment to Islamic practice and self-discipline; this goes way beyond prayer, positively impacting their lives in many ways.

- **Spiritual Guidance and Reflection:** Prayer allows Muslims to practice self-reflection and introspection. At prayer time, Muslims recite Qur'an verses and practice supplication, resulting in the Islamic messages and teachings becoming internalized and allowing for deep contemplation. Prayer not only gives Muslims the guidance they need but also acts as a kind of compass, helping them navigate all of life's challenges and choose the right path.

- **Spiritual Unity:** Congregational prayers help Muslims develop a sense of community and unity, particularly during the annual festivals and the Friday prayer. Praying with others helps promote a sense of brotherhood/sisterhood, spiritual solidarity, and a shared purpose.

Prayer draws Muslims closer to Allah (SWT) and allows them to develop a strong spiritual connection with the Divine to transform their lives. But spiritual benefits aren't the only ones Muslims gain from prayer.

Physical and Mental Benefits

Islamic prayer also brings several mental and physical benefits, including:

Physical Benefits:

- **Physical Exercise:** Islamic prayer requires believers to move – this means standing, bowing, sitting, and prostrating themselves before Allah (SWT). All of this is a gentle exercise form that helps promote flexibility and stretch their muscles.

- **Blood Circulation:** All of these movements promote healthy circulation of blood through the body. This helps prevent health issues caused by poor circulation and keeps their cardiovascular system strong.

- **Muscle Tone:** Because their prayer movements are repetitive and they have to hold certain postures, Muslims benefit from good muscle tone and stronger legs, back, core, and arms.

- **Flexible Joints:** Participating in regular prayer movements flexes the joints and extends them, thus strengthening flexibility. This also prevents the risk of conditions related to the joints and stiffness.

- **The Mind-Body Connection:** Mental focus and physical movements are in sync during prayer, and this helps Muslims develop a stronger mind-body connection. This helps promote mindfulness and body awareness.

Mental and Emotional Benefits:

- **Stress Relief:** Participation in regular prayer provides a break from the daily grind of life, therefore, giving a time of calm and relaxation. The focus and connection to the Divine can help relieve stress and decrease anxiety.

- **Presence and Mindfulness:** Islamic prayer requires Muslims to be present in the moment, focusing entirely on Allah (SWT). Practicing mindfulness helps calm the mind, slow all racing thoughts, increase clarity, and bring a sense of serenity and peace.

- **Regulating the Emotions:** Prayer allows Muslims a chance for introspection, self-reflection, and the opportunity to ask for forgiveness. It helps them regulate their emotions and promotes inner peace and well-being.

- **Spiritual Fulfillment:** Praying allows Muslims to fulfill their spiritual needs, gain a real sense of purpose, and promote a connection to a higher power. This contributes to better mental health and contentment.

- **Psychological:** Participating in regular prayer, including the rituals and recitation of Qur'an verses, can soothe the mind and uplift it, bringing hope, comfort, and guidance. This all has a positive impact on mental health.

- **Community Connection:** Congregational prayers unite worshippers in a shared space, providing a sense of social connection and community. This contributes to a sense of belonging and improves mental well-being.

While Islamic prayer provides these benefits, everyone will have a different experience and benefit differently. It's also important to note that these benefits can be impacted - negatively or positively – by the individual's sincerity and intention while praying.

Connection with Allah (SWT)

Islamic prayer is considered one of the strongest ways to connect directly with Allah (SWT). It provides the necessary channel for Muslims to seek guidance, closeness to the Divine, and spiritual fulfillment. Some of the benefits Muslims can reap include:

- **A Stronger Bond:** Prayer provides a deeper bond between Allah (SWT) and the individual. By participating in prayer, Muslims express their devotion, love, and gratitude toward Allah (SWT) and acknowledge their dependence on Him. This ensures a constant connection that strengthens the relationship and develops a better sense of closeness.

- **Asking for Guidance:** Prayer offers Muslims a way to ask Allah (SWT) for guidance. During prayer, Muslims supplicate for clarity, wisdom, and direction or guidance in life. They pass their concerns on to Allah (SWT), and show their trust in Him and ask for Divine guidance.

- **Comfort and Solace:** Prayer is a way for Muslims to find inner peace, comfort, and solace. They turn to Allah (SWT) when they are sad, distressed, or experiencing hardship, looking for support and solace.

Prayer provides a kind of refuge where Muslims can lay out their concerns and burdens and receive tranquility and reassurance in return.

- **Trust and Reliance:** Prayer is a way to develop a sense of reliance and trust in God. Allah (SWT) fulfills the spiritual and material needs, and by praying, Muslims acknowledge His mercy and power and His ability to answer those prayers.

- **Gratitude:** Islamic prayer allows Muslims to express gratitude to Allah (SWT), offering thanks for His provisions, blessings, and guidance. Using prayer to express gratitude helps them develop contentment, a positive mindset, and recognition of the continuous favors Allah (SWT) provides.

- **Forgiveness:** Prayer allows Muslims to ask for forgiveness and offer repentance. They acknowledge all their imperfections and ask Allah (SWT) for forgiveness for their shortcomings and sins. They also use this time to commit to working toward righteousness. Prayer gives them space for repentance, self-reflection, and commitment to spiritual growth.

- **Faith and Spirituality:** By participating in regular prayer, Muslims gain the chance to nourish their spirituality. It helps them develop a deep sense of devotion, faith, and connection. Prayer is a way for them to raise their consciousness and experience the worldly realm's supremacy.

- **Comprehensive Relationship:** Prayer covers several aspects of Islamic worship, including reciting various verses from the Qur'an, praise, supplication, and glorifying Allah (SWT). This complex approach allows Muslims to build a complete relationship with Allah (SWT), embracing hope, fear, love, and reverence.

Prayer offers Muslims many benefits, not least in their connection with Allah (SWT). It also provides physical, mental, emotional, and spiritual benefits, which goes some way toward explaining why it is such an important part of Muslim life.

Now that you understand the benefits of prayer, it's time to delve into the rituals and practices. The next chapter is the longest in the guide and is quite involved, filled with useful information and steps to help you understand the rituals of prayer.

Chapter 3: Rituals and Requirements of Prayer

Before we learn about the rituals and practices of prayer, we should look at the five daily prayers. The sun's position determines the prayer times, therefore, it varies from season to season and place to place. Most Muslim communities have a Mosque which publishes the prayer schedule. While it is considered best practice to start praying right after the published time, prayers are said to be on time, provided they start before the end of the prayer period.

The Five Daily Prayers

3. All Muslims are required to pray five times a day. Source: https://www.pexels.com/photo/muslim-black-man-praying-at-home-5996991/

These are the prayers:

- **Fajr:** The Dawn Prayer starts just before the sun begins to rise, as the light of dawn appears, and ends right before the official sunrise for the day. These prayers comprise two Rak'ahs (more about Rak'ah will be discussed later in the chapter), which is considered one of the most important prayers.

- **Dhuhr:** The Midday Prayer starts once the sun has passed its highest point and comprises four Rak'ahs.

- **Asr:** The Afternoon Prayer starts late afternoon and comprises four Rak'ahs – it must be completed before sunset.

- **Maghrib:** The Evening Prayer starts immediately after sunset and comprises three Rak'ahs.

- **Isha:** The Night Prayer starts once twilight has gone completely and comprises four Rak'ahs.

Before Prayer/Salah

Before starting the prayer process, Muslims must undergo certain rituals to ensure their spiritual, mental, and physical readiness. The most important part of this is a purification process called Wudu. If it is not performed for any reason, then neither your prayer will be complete, nor Allah (SWT) will accept the prayers.

"No salah is accepted without wudu."
Sahih Muslim, Book 2, Hadith 2

Here's how to do it:

4. *Ablution is necessary before every prayer. Source:*
https://unsplash.com/photos/DAnVHY9Wagk

Step One: Declare Your Intention

The first thing every Muslim must do is understand and declare their intention to perform Wudu. There are no specific words here; just be sure it comes from deep within your mind and heart and is pure.

Step Two: Say, Bismillah

This step must not be missed; before beginning, say the word "Bismillah." This means "In the name of Allah" and can be said aloud or to yourself.

Step Three: Wash Your Hands

Start with the right hand, as taught by the Prophet Muhammed (PBUH), and wash it thoroughly, ensuring the water touches you from the fingertips to the wrist. Do this three times on the right hand, then move to the left and do it all again.

Step Four: Rinse Your Mouth

Rinse your mouth using water taken from your right hand. Swish it around to rinse out your mouth; do it three times.

Step Five: Inhale Water into Your Nose

Again, scoop water into your right hand and "sniff" it into your nostrils. By this, I mean snort it in and then blow it back out. Again, this should be done three times, but be sure you don't inhale too much water; it could hurt you and do some damage.

Step Six: Wash Your Face

Clean your entire face thoroughly, ensuring each part between your forehead and chin is wet. If you have a beard, run your wet hands through it – it doesn't matter if it is long or short; this step must be done.

Step Seven: Wash Your Arms

As always, the right side is first, so wash your arm from your elbow down to your fingertips and repeat twice more. Do the same with the left arm.

Step Eight: Wipe Your Head

There's no need to soak your head in water. Run your wet hands across your head, go from your forehead to your neck, and come back the other way. You only need to do this once, and it doesn't matter whether you have no hair or a lot – the method is the same.

Step Nine: Clean Your Ears

Wet your right forefinger and thumb; move your finger in a circular motion around the ear canal and rub your thumb behind the ear. Do the same using the left forefinger and thumb for the left ear.

Step 10: Wash Your Feet

Now wipe your right foot up to the ankle, cleaning in between your toes. Do this twice more on the right foot and then do it three times on the left.

Step Eleven: Say the Shahada and One Dua

According to the Prophet Muhammed (PBUH), the Shahada below must be said once a Muslim has completed their Wudu:

"Ash-hadu an la ilaha illal lahu wa ash-hadu anna Muhammadan 'abduhu wa rasuluh."

In English:

"I testify that there is no god but Allah, and I also testify that Muhammad is His servant and messenger."

And the following dua:

"Allahuma j'alnee mina tawabeen waj-'alnee minal mutatahireen"

In English:

"O Allah, make me among those who seek repentance and make me among those who purify themselves."

The Wudu is done, and prayers can now start.

A Quick Checklist

Before you stand up to start praying, make sure you have completed the following checklist:

1. Complete Wudu

2. Check the time. Each prayer has a set time of day and are evenly spread to ensure a constant reminder of Allah (SWT).

3. Wear the right clothes. It is recommended that males wear long loose pants and a loose shirt, while females should wear a long loose dress that covers them. Their heads must also be covered. This is called "awrah."

4. Find a clean place to pray. If you don't pray in a mosque, you must find somewhere clean or use a carpet to cover the floor. You can also pray outside on concrete, sand, grass, etc.

5. Face the right direction — this means facing the Qibla, the direction of the Kaaba, from wherever you are.

Now you can pray.

How to Pray

Here are the steps you will follow during your prayer:

- Stand

- Takbir

- Surah al-Fatihah – recite the Qur'an verses

- Ruku - bow

- Sujud – prostrate yourself

- Tashahud – sit

Each prayer comprises one or more units or Rak'ahs, and each Rak'ah has these steps:

- Standing

- Reciting the relevant Qur'an verses

- Bowing

- Prostrating

Each prayer has a set number of Rak'ahs:

- **Fajr** – two Rak'ahs

- **Dhur** – four Rak'ahs

- **Asr** – four Rak'ahs

- **Maghrib -** three Rak'ahs

- **Isha** – four Rak'ahs

Here's how each Rak'ah is performed:

Step One

Before you begin praying, set your intention; it must come from the heart, and it must be an intention to pray to Allah

(SWT). Once you begin, you should be focused solely on the prayer – nothing else should be on your mind.

Step Two

Next, raise your hands to your ears and say, "Allahu Akbar." This is the official start of the prayer, and from now on, make sure you ignore distractions and keep your focus only on your prayer.

Step Three

Drop your hands and rest them over your belly button, in case of males, and put your hands on your chest, in case of females. Left hand first, with the right hand placed on top.

Step Four

Focus your vision on the ground before you. According to the Prophet Muhammed (PBUH), your eyes should always be focused on where you will prostrate. And while there is no obligation to do this, recommendations say that you should read the dua below after you have said "Allahu Akbar."

"Subhanakal-lahumma wabihamdika
watabarakas-muka
wataa 'ala jadduka
wala ilaha ghayruka."

In English:

"How perfect you are, O Allah. I praise you
How blessed is Your name
How lofty is Your position
And none has the right to be worshipped but You"

Step Five

Next is the Surah al-Fatihah (the Qur'an's initial chapter) and this is the first line:

"A'auodu billaahi minash-shaytaanir rajeem"

In English:

"I seek refuge in Allah from the accursed Shaytan (devil)."

The remaining words to recite are:

"Bismillaahir ar-Rahmani ar-RaheemAl hamdu lillaahi rabbil 'alameen
Ar-Rahmani ar-Raheem
Maaliki yawmid deen
Iyyaaka na'aboodu wa iyyaaka nasta'een
Ihdeenas siraatal mustaqeem
Siraatal ladheena an 'amta' alayhim
Ghayril maghduubi' alayhim waladawleen"

In English:

"In the name of God, the infinitely Compassionate and Merciful.
Praise be to Allah, Lord of all the worlds.
The Most Gracious, the Most Merciful.
Master on the Day of Recompense (Judgement Day).
You alone do we worship, and You alone do we ask for help.
Guide us on the straight path,
The path of those who You have bestowed favor, not of those who have evoked [Your] anger or of those who are astray."

When you have finished reciting Surah al-Fatihah, follow with another verse from the Qur'an that fits the prayer and your intention. However, you must recite the Surah al-Fatihah in every Rak'ah:

- If there are two Rak'ahs in the prayer, start with Surah al-Fatihah, followed by another Surah in both the Ra'kah.

- If there are three Rak'ahs in the prayer, say the Surah al-Fatihah, followed by another Surah in the first two Ra'kah. However, in the third Rak'ah you only recite Surah al-Fatihah.

- If there are four Rak'ahs in the prayer, say the Surah Fatihah, followed by another Surah in the first two Rak'ah. However, in the third and fourth Rak'ah, only recite Surah al-Fatihah.

Step Six

Next is Ruku, which is the bowed position. Standing tall, focus on the spot where you will go into Sujud (prostration) in a later step. While bending forward, with your back straight, drop your hands onto your knees, and say *"Allahu Akbar."* When you are in the Ruku position, say the following line thrice:

"Subhanna rabbeeyal adheem"

In English:

"How perfect is my Lord, the Magnificent"

Step Seven

While getting back up, let your hands drop to your sides, and say:

"Samea Allahu leman hameeda"

English translation:

"Allah hears those who praise him"

When you are back in a fully upright position, say:

"Rabbanna walak alhamd"

English Translation:

"Our Lord, to You is all praise"

Step Eight

Next is Sujud. This is the prostration position; drop to your knees saying, "Allahu Akbar." Lean forward, hands flat on the floor, and slide forward, dipping your head down to touch your forehead and nose to the floor. Keep your forearms off the floor.

Step Nine

Say the following line thrice while in Sujud:

"Subhanna rabby al'alaa"

English Translation:

"How perfect is my Lord, the Most High"

Step Ten

Move back to a sitting position while saying "Allahu Akbar" again. Sit down with your left leg tucked beneath you (you should be sitting on it), and your left foot should be on the floor. Your right foot should be upright, with your toes touching the floor and your hands resting on your knees. From this position, you will seek forgiveness from Allah (SWT). The dua below is optional:

"Rab ighfir lee"

In English:

"O my Lord, forgive me."

Step Eleven

Repeat the ninth step for another Sujud and repeat the following three times:

Subhanna rabbeeyal 'alaa

Step Twelve:

Lift yourself back into a standing position, saying *"Allahu Akbar"* as you do.

Those are the steps needed for a single Rak'ah, which must be completed during every prayer. Where there are more than two Rak'ahs, the third is a tashahud, which is the thirteenth step.

Step Thirteen

When you have completed the second Sujud, sit back up, lift your right index finger and recite:

*"Al Tahiyyaatu lilaahi wa Salawaatu wat tayibaatu
Assalaamu 'alaika ayyuhan nabiyyu wa rahmatu Allahi
wa barakaatuh
Assalaamu 'alaynaa wa 'alaa 'ebaadillaahis saaliheen,
Ash hadu allaa ilaha illa Allah Wa ash hadu anna
Muhammadan 'abduhuu wa rasuuluh"*

In English:

*"All compliments, prayers and pure words are due to Allah.
Peace be upon you, O Prophet, and the mercy of Allah and His blessings.
Peace be upon us, and on the righteous slaves of Allah.
I bear witness that none has the right to be worshipped except Allah, and I bear witness that Muhammad is His slave and Messenger"*

If there are no more Rak'ahs to come, finish with this:

*"Allahumma salli 'ala Muhammadin wa 'ala aali
Muhammad
Kamaa salayta 'ala Ibraaheem wa 'ala aali Ibrahim
Innaka Hameedun Majeed
Wa baarik 'ala Muhammadin wa 'ala aali Muhammad
Kamaa baarakta 'ala Ibraaheem wa 'ala aali Ibrahim
Innaka Hameedun Majeed"*

English translation:

*"O Allah, send prayers upon Muhammad and upon the
family (or followers) of Muhammad, Just as You sent
prayers upon Ibrahim and the family (or followers) of
Ibrahim,
Verily, you are full of Praise and Majesty.
O Allah, bless Muhammad and the family (or followers)
of Muhammad as You blessed Ibrahim and the family (or
followers) of Ibraaheem,
Verily, you are full of Praise and Majesty."*

Tasleem

After saying the second bit of the tashahud, you must say
the tasleem – look to your right shoulder and say the
following:

Assalamu alaykum wa rahmatu Allah

Which translates to:

*May you be safe from evil, and Mercy of Allah be upon
you*

Turn and then look at your left shoulder and repeat it.

This brings the prayer to an end.

That was one Rak'ah or unit; simply combine two, three, or four as required for each prayer. Not all prayers are said aloud, though:

- **Fajr** – loudly
- **Dhur** – silently
- **Asr** – silently
- **Maghrib** – loudly for the first two Rak'ah and silently for the third
- **Isha** – loudly for the first two, silently for the last two

Chapter 4: Understanding the Components of Prayer

Knowing what to say, when, and how are important, but you also need to understand the components of a Salah. These were all mentioned in the last chapter, so I will go over them briefly here, just to cement them in your mind:

5.   *There are several components of prayer that every Muslim should know to pray correctly. Source:*
https://www.pexels.com/photo/woman-praying-on-a-prayer-mat-with-her-eyes-closed-8758358/

1. **Standing** – Otherwise known as Qiyam, every prayer begins with you standing tall, facing toward the Kaaba in Mecca. This is the Qibla or direction of prayer. You must stand with your feet shoulder-width apart, your hands resting loosely at your sides, and focus solely on your intention. Hold a straight posture, distribute your weight evenly between your feet, and keep your eyes focused on where you will prostrate yourself. Always show humility and attentiveness.

2. **Takbeer** – You start your prayer by saying *"Allahu Akbar,"* a declaration that Allah (SWT) is the greatest. This transitions you from the distractions and concerns in your life to the act of prayer, which is considered sacred by all Muslims. Put simply, it indicates a change in your focus and mindset toward worship.

3. **Recite Surah Al-Fatiha** – This is the opening chapter of the Qur'an and is the most important. It is recited in all Rak'ahs and is for guidance and to recognize Allah's (SWT) sovereignty. You will recite this silently unless otherwise indicated in the specific prayer.

4. **Bowing** – Also called Ruku, once you have recited the Surah al-Fatihah, you bend forward, lay your hands on your knees, and say "Subhanna rabbeeyal adheem" at least three times. This position is an indication of humility. Keep your back straight at all times.

5. **Prostration** – This is the Sujud position; lower yourself to your knees with your toes touching the ground. Lean forward and touch your hands, nose, and forehead to the floor – these five parts of your body MUST be touching the floor during Sujud; otherwise, it is not valid. There are two Sujud in every Rak'ah, and when you prostrate, say *"Subhanna rabby al' alaa"* three times. This is

considered the most humble of all the prayer positions and it is when you are closest to Allah (SWT). Ask for His blessings, forgiveness, and mercy.

6. **Sitting** – Also called Jalsa, when you finish the prostration, you sit for a short time in this position. Sit upright, your legs folded beneath you and rest on your left foot. This allows you to rest for a moment and makes the transition easy from one prostration to the next.

7. **Standing** – Also called Qa'dah, you rise from sitting and prepare for the next Rak'ah or finish the prayer altogether, depending on how many Rak'ahs are required.

8. **Second Prostration** – You enter a second prostration, the same as the first one. Again, you recite *"Subhanna rabby al' alaa"* three times. Doing this a second time reinforces your submission to Allah (SWT) and your complete devotion.

9. **Tashahud** – Once the second prostration is complete, sit in the Tashahud position. Your right foot should be upright, resting on its toes, while the left is flat on the floor. Recite the Shahada and any other required supplications and blessings.

10. **Salutations** – Known as Salam and Tasleem, you turn to face the right shoulder, saying, *"Assalamu alaykum wa rahmatu Allah."* Turn to the left shoulder and repeat. The prayer is now ended.

This is a general overview of how Islamic prayer is structured, but you should seek definitive guidance from knowledgeable individuals if you are new to this.

Chapter 5: Enhancing the Quality of Prayer

Every Muslim wants to be close to Allah (SWT) regardless of their level of belief. They work towards connecting more deeply with Him, and their daily consistent worship helps them do this. They also work to improve the quality of their prayer by ensuring their prayers are more meaningful. Here are some ways that you can enhance the quality of your Salah:

6. *Understanding why we pray and how to concentrate makes the process more meaningful. Source: https://www.pexels.com/photo/close-up-shot-of-person-holding-prayer-beads-7957066/*

1. **Understand the Meaning of Salah:** Salah will mean much more when you understand what you are reciting. Learn what the Arabic supplications and verses mean, and your connection with Allah (SWT) will deepen, and your focus will increase during prayer.

2. **Mindfulness and Concentration:** Learn to be mindful and use it during your prayers. Focus on every aspect of the prayer, avoid all distractions, and make sure your mind is completely clear of everything except your intention. Salah allows you to communicate directly with Allah (SWT), so make sure it has your attention and concentrate solely on your positions, movements, and recitations.

3. **Punctual and Consistent:** Pray on time daily to ensure a regular Salah routine. Offering Salah consistently helps you develop a disciplined mindset and a stronger connection with Allah (SWT). Unless it is absolutely necessary, do not delay or miss your prayer times and try to keep your schedule consistent.

4. **Improve your Recitations:** You might struggle if Arabic is not your first language. Take the time to learn and improve your recitations. You can enhance the beauty of your recitation by learning Tajweed, the rules of Qur'anic recitation, which also helps to understand what you are reciting better.

5. **Connect with the Qur'an:** Before you begin Salah, create a spiritual connection by reciting Qur'an verses or reading the translation. Reflect on what you recite and work towards implementing the teachings throughout your life. By connecting with the Qur'an in this way, your Salah will be deeper, more sincere, and more meaningful.

6. **Cultivate Khushu':** Khushu' should be cultivated during Salah as it involves reverence, humility, and complete focus. Khushu' is devotion and humility, and you must remember that you stand before Allah (SWT) and focus on cultivating a sense of gratitude and awe. Do not rush your prayer, and take the time to connect sincerely with Allah (SWT).

7. **Personal Du'as and Supplications:** Use your own du'as during your Salah. Once the obligatory prayers are finished, take the time for extra supplications, seeking Allah's (SWT) guidance, blessings, and forgiveness. Don't be afraid to pour out your heart, express your needs and desires, and ask for His guidance and mercy.

8. **Seek Spiritual Growth and Knowledge:** You should continuously seek knowledge about Salah and its aspects. Learn the prayer-related etiquette, virtues, and acts and attend lectures, seek guidance from others, or read Islamic books to boost your spiritual growth. The more you learn, the more enriched your Salah will be.

9. **Be Prepared for Salah:** Ensure your environment is conducive. Go through the Wudu steps, wear the correct attire, and make sure you are somewhere quiet and clean. This will ensure your mindset is right and helps you focus better.

10. **Seek Spiritual Purification:** Ask for forgiveness for your sins, repent, and purify your heart. Clear all negativity and distractions from your mind before your Salah. When you repent and ask for forgiveness regularly, you strengthen your spiritual state and bring more tranquility to your Salah.

11. **Slow Down:** Don't rush through your Salah. There is a lot to it, so take your time with each movement and

position and allow the peace and tranquility of each one to wash over you. Your concentration and focus are improved when you move slowly and consciously.

12. **Reflect on Allah's (SWT) Names and Attributes:** During your Salah, take the time to reflect on all of Allah's (SWT) names and attributes mentioned throughout the Qur'an. Contemplate His compassion, mercy, power, and wisdom. These reflections will help deepen your connection and increase your gratitude and humility while praying.

13. **Go to Congregational Prayers:** While praying alone is fine, you should make an effort to go to congregational prayers whenever you can, particularly the obligatory prayers. Praying with a congregation helps develop a sense of community and unity and helps you learn from others. It also helps your devotion and focus as you follow the Imam's movements and recitation.

14. **Recite Extra Supplications:** Memorize extra supplication from the Prophetic traditions (Sunnah) and recite them at different times during the Salah, for example, in the standing position after you recite from the Qur'an, before your prayer is concluded or while prostrating. Adding extra ones will add more meaning and depth to your Salah and help you speak your personal needs while you ask Allah (SWT) for blessings.

15. **Reflect on the Purpose of Prayer:** Prayer is not just physical; it also benefits you spiritually and helps you improve. Reflect on the purpose to help you seek a closer relationship with Allah (SWT), purify your soul, and ask for blessings and guidance. Doing this will add more devotion and intention to your prayer.

16.**Seek Guidance from Islamic Scholars:** If you have questions or doubts about Salah or an individual aspect, don't be afraid to ask for help. Speak to Islamic scholars and other knowledgeable people to get the right information. They have the expertise to help you understand Salah and practice it in the right way.

17.**Perform Sunnah Prayers Consistently:** This is in addition to obligatory prayers. Sunnah prayers are voluntary and come before and after the obligatory ones. Maintaining consistency can be incredibly rewarding and can deepen your connection with Allah (SWT). Establish a good habit of offering Sunnah prayers and increase your mindfulness and devotion to Allah (SWT).

Salah must be approached with devotion, sincerity, and the desire to make a connection with Allah (SWT). The suggestions above can help you enhance your Salah and experience its spiritual benefits.

Chapter 6: Common Questions and Misconceptions

Misconceptions can arise with just about anything, especially religion, and Islam is no different. To start this chapter, we'll deal with some of the more common ones before answering some of the commonly asked questions about Salah.

7. *Learning about the essence of prayer helps you disregard any misconceptions you might have. Source: https://www.pexels.com/photo/man-in-white-thobe-bowing-down-on-red-and-blue-rug-7129545/*

Common Misconceptions

1. Salah is only a physical ritual

Salah certainly involves a lot of physical movement, and some call it a form of exercise. However, it goes way beyond that. Salah is a complex worship ritual combining those physical actions with reciting verses from the Qur'an, supplications, and providing a deep spiritual connection between the individual and Allah (SWT). In short, it is a way of developing mindfulness, attaining spiritual purification, and seeking a closer relationship with Allah (SWT).

2. Quantity trumps quality

Salah's focus should be on quality and not quantity. Yes, Muslims must pray five times a day, but they don't have to go beyond the obligatory prayers if they don't want to. Quality means performing Salah with humility, total concentration, and understanding, even if the individual doesn't add in many voluntary prayers. Rushing the prayers or adding in loads of extra ones without practicing mindfulness can reduce the spiritual benefits.

3. A person must have a perfect external appearance

Being clean and wearing the right clothing is certainly important, but being sincere in intention and having a pure state of heart is far more important. Internal focus, devotion, and humility are critical during Salah; having a sincere, pure heart is far more important than focusing solely on external appearance.

4. Women aren't allowed to pray during menstruation

It is a common misconception that they are not allowed to pray. Instead, Islamic law allows them to be exempt from prayer during menstruation and if they have postnatal bleeding. This is based on the rule that prevents discomfort to any individual and maintains cleanliness. Once the bleeding stops, the women may resume their regular prayer schedule.

5. Salah is obligatory only in Arabic

While Salah should be performed in Arabic, it is only to the extent that an individual can do it. This is because it preserves the Qur'an's words and Prophetic traditions. However, it is as important to understand the intentions and meaning behind the recitations. While it is important to learn Arabic, it is also important the understand the basic meaning behind each recitation to build a strong connection with Allah (SWT) and a better spiritual experience.

6. Salah may only be performed in certain locations

Performing Salah in a mosque is preferable, but it can be done anywhere. The only rules are that the place is clean and quiet. Islam promotes flexibility in Salah; each person can choose whether to attend a mosque or pray at work, home, school, or any other location. The focus is on creating a connection with Allah (SWT) and finding an environment conducive to devotion and focus.

Misconceptions can arise for many reasons, mostly due to a lack of knowledge. Seeking guidance from genuine Islamic scholars and continuously learning is the only way to ensure you understand Salah and perform it according to Islamic teachings.

Commonly Asked Questions

1. What is the Purpose of Salah in Islam?

Salah has a multifaceted purpose in Islam. It is a complex form of worship that gives Muslims a chance to connect with Allah (SWT), ask for his guidance and forgiveness, and express their gratitude. Salah is a way of attaining spiritual purification, developing humility and mindfulness, and building a strong relationship with Allah (SWT).

2. Why Must Muslims Pray Five Times Daily?

This is an obligation that Allah (SWT) ordained. The five daily prayers are a way of keeping Allah (SWT) constantly in mind and worshipping Him regularly. The prayers also allow Muslims to show gratitude, reflect, and ask for Divine help in every aspect of their lives.

3. How Is Salah Different From Prayers in Other Religions?

Salah has a distinct structure, specific recitations, and postures and is comprehensive in its nature. Physical movements, intentions, supplications, and recitations are all included, and Salah is focused on submitting to Allah's (SWT) will, asking for His mercy, and aligning with His guidance.

4. Why Are the Physical Postures and Movements in Salah Significant?

They are significant because they offer physical, spiritual, and psychological benefits. These movements symbolize humility, gratitude, and submission to Allah (SWT), and all the different positions put together are complex expressions of a Muslim's devotion; they allow the individual to engage their mind, body, and soul in worship.

5. Why Must Salah Be Done Facing Kaaba in Mecca?

Muslims face Kaaba because it is a unified direction of prayer. It represents the Muslim community's unity and is a symbol of the center of worship for Muslims worldwide. When they face the Kaaba, it reminds them of Allah's (SWT) oneness and the interconnectivity of the global Muslim community.

6. Are Non-Muslims Allowed to Observe or Participate in Salah?

Non-Muslims are always welcome to observe Salah, but they may not participate as this requires them to adhere to Islamic practices and beliefs. They may attend mosques as observers, giving them an idea of the practices and rituals within the Islamic faith.

7. How Does Salah Contribute to a Muslim's Well-Being and Spiritual Growth?

Salah allows Muslims to cultivate discipline, develop mindfulness, ask for forgiveness, and strengthen their faith. When Muslims engage in Salah regularly and sincerely, they can find solace, peace, and guidance through their relationship with the Almighty, leading to them living a more conscious, virtuous way of life.

8. What Are the Steps to Salah?

Performing Salah requires several steps, including:

- Wudu – ritual purification

- Facing the Kaaba

- Reciting different verses from the Qur'an

- Different physical positions, including standing, bowing, and prostrating themselves.

- Making their personal supplications

The practice ends with salutations, but these steps may vary, depending on which of the five prayers they participate in.

9. Is Salah Prohibited at Any Specific Times or Under Certain Conditions?

Yes, there are certain times when Salah cannot be performed, known as 'times of prevention" or "prohibited times." These times include the time of sunrise to when the sun is fully risen – this takes about 15 to 20 minutes after sunrise. It also includes the period between noon and when the sun starts to set and between sunset and when the sky no longer has any traces of redness. Salah can be performed at any time other than these.

10. How Do You Learn the Correct Way to Perform Salah, and in Arabic?

This is best done by seeking help from qualified Islamic scholars, attending Islamic courses or classes, studying genuine Islamic resources, observing experienced and knowledgeable Muslims during Salah, emulating them, and learning Arabic. Attend any mosque or Muslim community, and someone will be willing to show you the ropes.

11. Is Understanding Arabic Necessary for Effective Salah?

Understanding Arabic is not necessary for Salah to be effective, but it certainly helps if you can understand the meanings and learn some basic Arabic recitations. When you can understand the meanings behind the supplications and verses, you can enhance your spiritual experience and connect more deeply with the words being spoken.

12. Are There Specific or Recommended Verses or Supplications to Recite?

Yes. Certain verses must be spoken without exception, but there are also additional verses and supplications you can recite too, such as Nafl and Sunnah prayers. These will depend on personal preference and the specific prayer.

13. Can Salah Be Performed Alone, Or Should It Be Congregational?

Salah can certainly be performed alone, although praying in a congregation is better. Muslims are urged to attend a mosque as often as possible but are also encouraged to make Salah their own. Friday prayer is obligatory, and all male Muslims must attend it.

14. What Role Does Intention Play in Salah?

Intention, or niyyah, is critical to Salah because it is how Muslims convey their sincerity and the purpose behind their worship. The intentions should be set right before Salah and must come from the heart. The intention must be aligned for Allah's (SWT) sake, fulfilling obligations and seeking Allah's (SWT) pleasure.

15. How Do You Keep Your Focus During Salah and Ignore Distractions?

This is quite challenging, but there are some things you can do to help. Find somewhere secluded and quiet to perform Salah, reflect on what the recitations mean, learn the proper pronunciations so you can recite and understand the Qur'an, and learn mindfulness.

16. What Should a Muslim Do if They Cannot Perform a Salah on Time or Miss One?

Any missed or later Salahs should be made up for as soon as possible, and forgiveness must be sought from Allah (SWT). Missed prayers must be performed in their entirety, including all the recitations and physical actions. It's best to set a routine and stick to the designated times for the prayers; attending congregational prayers can help with this.

17. Are Women Allowed to Pray With Men in Congregations, or Lead Salah?

Islamic tradition dictates that women are allowed to lead all-female congregational prayers. However, in mixed gatherings, it is more common for men to lead Salah, and women are actively encouraged to pray in their rows or behind the men to minimize distractions and preserve modesty.

18. How Is Salah Connected to Other Parts of Islamic Daily Life and Worship?

Salah is considered the primary building block of Islamic worship, connecting with all aspects of a Muslim's life. It is a way to purify oneself, ask for sins to be forgiven, align actions with Islamic teachings, and develop self-control, humility, discipline, and gratitude. Salah is connected with other worship acts, such as charitable donations and acts, fasting, and good character; thus, it is the basis of a righteous, balanced life.

Chapter 7: Overcoming Challenges in Prayer

Being fully focused and concentrating on Salah is important because it can deepen your spiritual experience and connection to Allah (SWT). However, this is sometimes easier said than done; external distractions, a busy mind, and challenges in life all get in the way. Focus and concentration are key elements, so I'll start by talking about why you need them during Salah:

8.   *There are certain things you can do to overcome any challenges you might face when it comes to prayer. Source: https://unsplash.com/photos/iQWvVYMtv1k*

1. **To Fulfill the Purpose:** Salah is more than a physical practice; it also helps Muslims reach spiritual purification and gain a closer relationship with Allah (SWT). Concentration helps them engage their minds, souls, and hearts fully in the worship, fulfilling Salah's real purpose.

2. **To Increase Spiritual Awareness:** Maintaining concentration and focus during Salah allows Muslims to gain more spiritual awareness, leading to them experiencing a better presence and connection with Allah (SWT). It also helps their experience of humility, submission, and gratitude toward Allah (SWT) become more profound.

3. **To Enhance Reflection and Focus:** Solid concentration helps them maintain focus on recitations, understand what they mean, and reflect on the Qur'an's messages. Muslims can internalize Salah's teachings, allowing personal growth and spiritual enlightenment.

4. **To Strengthen Their Relationship with Allah (SWT):** Muslims strive for a deep, personal connection with Allah (SWT), and Salah provides that opportunity. This is a time for them to talk with Allah (SWT) and ask for His forgiveness, mercy, and guidance. With focus and concentration, their relationship becomes more sincere and intimate, and they can develop solace, peace, and trust in Allah's (SWT) presence.

What happens if you don't pay attention during Salah? What if you allow your mind to wander? Lack of concentration during Salah does have some adverse effects:

1. **Spiritual Neglect:** If your focus and concentration are missing in Salah, it can result in your approach to worship becoming mechanical and superficial, resulting in your spiritual growth coming to a halt. It can also stop you from creating a strong connection with Allah (SWT), and any connection you do manage to develop will have very little meaning.

2. **A Decrease in Devotion:** When you perform Salah with less focus and concentration than you should, it becomes nothing more than a physical exercise with no real meaning; the spiritual essence will be missing, leading to a decrease in your devotion and a collapse in your connection with Allah (SWT).

3. **Missed Opportunities:** Salah is one of the best opportunities to ask Allah (SWT) for guidance, blessings, and forgiveness. When you don't concentrate, you risk missing out on the spiritual benefits and rewards Salah brings.

For some people, this lack of concentration is borne of laziness, a tendency to procrastinate rather than throw themselves wholeheartedly into the act. There are some ways to help you overcome this:

1. **Understand Why Salah Is Important:** If you truly understand why Salah is significant and how it impacts your spiritual, physical, and mental well-being, you will no longer struggle to prioritize it in your life.

2. **Get into a Routine:** Set up and adhere to a Salah routine. Make it a regular part of your life, and get into the habit of attending daily prayers. Set a schedule, allocate set times of the day for Salah, and it

will slowly become a regular part of your life, one you won't want to miss.

3. **Seek Accountability:** When you pray alone, it can be all too easy to start missing sessions or questioning why you need to do it. Get together with your family or friends or attend congregational prayers to help make yourself accountable and motivate you to pray regularly with more dedication and devotion.

4. **Think about the Rewards:** Remind yourself regularly of the blessings and rewards of regular, sincere prayer. Think about the spiritual benefits, and you'll find yourself inspired and motivated to throw yourself into it with all your heart.

How do you deal with distractions? How do you stay consistent and focused on Salah, shutting out everything else around you and in your mind?

1. **Set Up the Right Environment:** This is especially the case for newly converted Muslims or those who haven't been brought up with the daily rituals of prayer. Find somewhere quiet and peaceful to pray, somewhere without distractions to take your mind off Salah. If you pray at home, set aside a specific area, and ensure it is clean, quiet, and free of electronic devices, noises, and any other potential disturbances.

2. **Seek Refuge in Allah (SWT):** Before you start Salah, take refuge in Allah (SWT) and ask Him to protect you from distractions. This will help you focus on the act and dismiss all unnecessary thoughts and distractions.

3. **Focus on What the Recitations Mean:** When you can focus on understanding what the recitations mean and reflect on the actual words, it can help you

maintain concentration and stop your mind from being taken over by other things.

4. **Learn Mindfulness:** Develop mindfulness by ensuring you are present in the moment throughout Salah. Be fully aware of every position, posture, movement, and word you recite. Focus your mind solely on the worship and your connection to Allah (SWT).

5. **Seek Perseverance and Patience:** Ignoring distractions, keeping your mind clear of everything but worship, and consistency takes great patience and perseverance. You must learn to acknowledge that there will always be some distractions, and that is normal, but you can learn to minimize them by putting in the effort and ensuring your intention is sincere.

These tips can help you to increase your concentration and focus on your worship, stop yourself from getting lazy in your practice, and help you deal with distractions. Consistency is key, but you need strong commitment, building up regular prayer habits, and understanding the spiritual benefits of Salah. Combine this with regularly asking Allah ((SWT) for forgiveness and guidance, and you'll soon find yourself overcoming the challenges during Salah.

Chapter 8: Prayer in Daily Life

The five daily prayers are an integral and essential part of daily Muslim life, not to mention one of the five pillars of Islam. But why is prayer so important to Muslims? What does it bring into their lives?

9.   *Praying is one of the five pillars of Islam. Source:*
https://unsplash.com/photos/tiZXFz4YdYc

1. **A Connection with Allah (SWT):** Prayer is a way for Muslims to communicate with Allah (SWT), a

peaceful worship act, and a way for them to show obedience and submission to their Creator. Participating in the five daily prayers allows them to confirm their strong belief in the oneness of Allah (SWT) and acknowledge their dependence on Him.

2. **Nurturing the Spirit:** Prayers nourish the soul and pave the way for a personal connection with Allah (SWT). Daily prayers allow Muslims to find tranquility and inner peace and give them a sense of purpose. Each prayer is a kind of battery, providing a recharge for the spirit and gently reminding every individual of their role in life.

3. **Self-Control and Discipline:** Muslims can build self-control and discipline through regular participation in daily prayers. Salah requires them to set specific time aside throughout the day and give their religious matters precedence over everything else. Building this discipline helps them develop great time management skills and a balanced lifestyle.

4. **Gratitude and Remembrance:** The five daily prayers allow Muslims the opportunity to remember Allah (SWT) continuously and express their gratitude for His blessings. It reminds them that their lives are filled with blessings and helps them develop a sense of humility and gratitude. Prayer also allows them to express their thanks for Allah's (SWT) provision, mercy, and guidance.

5. **Unity and Community:** Prayers are also important in developing a sense of community and unity among Muslims. When they join together to pray, their bond is strengthened, and they have a sense of

togetherness. It also allows them to interact socially, offer support to one another, and worship collectively.

6. **Ethical and Moral Development:** Prayer is more than just the physical actions of bowing and prostration. It also allows much-needed time for self-evaluation and spiritual reflection. During Salah, verses from the Qur'an are recited as a way for Muslims to ask forgiveness for their sins and weaknesses and to pray for guidance. The practice brings about ethical and moral development and encourages Muslims to work toward a virtuous and righteous life.

The five daily prayers are a duty and a way for Muslims to develop a deep, spiritual connection with their God. It helps them develop a strong bond with Him and maintain it, leading to a balanced life based firmly on the principles and teachings of Islam. Prayer provides Muslims with a source of tranquility and guidance. The importance of prayer is emphasized throughout the Qur'an, and its role in providing peace of mind and spiritual guidance is highlighted. One example of this is Surah Al-Baqarah(2:45), where Allah says:

"Seek help through patience and prayer. Indeed, Allah is with the patient."

This verse tells us that prayer is important for helping and guiding Muslims, and when times are difficult, they can use prayer to seek solace. It tells them that praying supports them and that Allah (SWT) shadows and help them where He thinks it is needed.

The Hadith literature also provides many of the Prophet Muhammed's (PBUH) authentic sayings that emphasize the importance of Salah. One Hadith that Abdullah ibn Mas'ud narrated says:

"The coolness of my eyes has been placed in the prayer."
(Sunan An-Nasa'i)

This Hadith signifies that prayer provides the Prophet's (PBUH) heart with tranquility and comfort and is a source of inner peace and solace. It is a reflection of the spiritual connection the Prophet (PBUH) experienced as he prayed.

One of the important ways daily prayer helps Muslims is by developing self-discipline. Participating in the five daily prayers requires consistency and commitment, and Muslims must be able to stick to a schedule. Doing this promotes self-discipline in several ways:

1. **Time Management:** Daily prayer requires effective time management; five daily prayers means Muslims have to organize their day around the five prayer timings. This encourages the prioritization of their religious obligations and ensures their time is allocated efficiently; this results in a more disciplined approach to managing time.

2. **Commitment and Consistency:** Praying regularly throughout the day requires commitment and consistency. No matter the external distractions or personal circumstances, Muslims must work towards punctuality in terms of their prayer obligations. This leads to self-discipline, encourages perseverance, and develops a sense of responsibility toward their religious duties.

3. **Leaving Procrastination Behind:** Praying regularly can help individuals leave their tendencies to procrastinate. Because the five daily prayers must be recited at set times, Muslims learn not to neglect or delay them. When prompt prayers become a habit, it

can lead to more productivity and a better, more proactive mindset in other areas of their lives.

4. **Concentration and Focus:** Islamic prayer requires full concentration and focus on the connection with Allah (SWT). While performing Salah, distractions must be kept to a minimum, allowing Muslims to engage in the positions, recitations, and supplications; this leads to better mental discipline and concentration skills that can be used in other work and living areas.

5. **Self-Control and Willpower:** When Muslims participate in regular prayer, it teaches them how to exercise self-control and willpower. They may have to rise early in the morning for the first prayer, abstain from anything unrelated to prayer during the prayer timings, and set aside social time to pray. Adhering to these requirements consistently helps Muslims resist temptation and build up their self-control and self-discipline in other areas of life.

Regular prayer is an excellent way of building self-discipline. Prayer is a reminder of how to leave procrastination behind, practice effective time management and consistency, improve concentration and focus, and have more self-control and willpower. Participating in daily prayers helps Muslims lead more productive, disciplined lives.

In the final chapter, we'll look at prayer as a spiritual journey.

Chapter 9: Prayer as a Spiritual Journey

Islam is more than just a religion; it is also a spiritual journey encompassing a complex way of life that helps individuals travel a well-worn path of spiritual development, encouraging personal growth and creating a close connection with Allah (SWT). Islam teaches us that humans are dual in their nature – they have a physical body and a spiritual soul; it also teaches us that developing the soul and nurturing it is of considerable importance.

10.   *It's important to remember that prayer in Islam is part of the spiritual journey. Source: https://unsplash.com/photos/asEF6JoLZ44*

Islamic prayer, or Salah, is of huge importance to all Muslims and is considered the most profound of all spiritual journeys; it is a way for individuals to create a deep connection and communicate with Allah (SWT). Islamic prayer isn't just physical. It also involves the worshipper's inner state and creates harmony between the mind, body, and soul.

The spiritual journey of Islam begins with niyyah, the intention to create a connection with Allah (SWT) to ask for His forgiveness, mercy, and guidance. The intention sets the stage, allowing the worshipper to enter a fully focused state of mindfulness and devotion.

Muslims prepare for this journey by performing Wudu – a cleansing and purification ritual to clean the body and mind and remove all worldly distractions. This prepares them to stand before their Creator.

When the prayer begins, Qur'an verses are recited to glorify and praise Allah (SWT). These words help remind Muslims of Allah's (SWT) attributes; of the importance His presence holds in the worshipper's life. When they recite the verses, their minds and hearts are attuned to Allah (SWT), developing a sense of awe, humility, and gratitude.

The prayer also involves physical movements, but these are more than just exercises; they also help manifest their surrender and submission to Allah's (SWT) will. Each movement is spiritually significant, giving the worshipper a chance to holistically engage their body, mind, and soul. These movements also allow to express gratitude, devotion, and reliance on God as they ask for His mercy and guidance.

While performing the physical movements, the worshipper's mind is focused on remembering Allah (SWT). They recite praises, supplications, and prayers to help increase their mindfulness of His presence in their lives, developing a deep spiritual connection at the same time.

Islamic prayer also allows for self-correction and self-reflection, serving as a time for introspection and allowing the individual to evaluate their intentions, actions, and character, asking for forgiveness for their sins and resolving to self-improve. Muslims use repentance to find spiritual purification, asking Allah (SWT) for forgiveness and mercy for their transgressions, conscious and unconscious.

The congregational prayers bring Muslims together on a spiritual journey, developing a sense of solidarity, community, and equality and reinforcing that all believers are treated equally before Allah (SWT), regardless of their worldly possessions or social status.

But the spiritual journey goes much further than the times and places of prayer; it also significantly influences mindset and conduct throughout every Muslim's life. The lessons they learn during the prayers – gratitude, patience, humility, and reliance – are their guiding force, helping them get through life's challenges, making the right decisions, and strengthening their bond with Allah (SWT).

Here's a look at what makes Islamic prayer a spiritual journey, point by point:

1. **A Closer Connection with Allah (SWT):** Islamic prayer's spiritual journey is ultimately about creating and strengthening a connection with Allah (SWT). It is a way to seek divine love, intimacy, and closeness with Him. Muslims work towards developing a relationship built on devotion, trust, and surrender. Their journey involves constantly asking for forgiveness, self-reflection, and aligning their intentions and actions with the Divine. This

brings tranquility, peace, and spiritual fulfillment to their lives.

2. **Self-Control and Spiritual Discipline:** Islamic prayer instills self-control and discipline in worshippers. Sticking to specific conditions and times for prayer helps them learn to prioritize religious obligations over everything else, but this discipline spills over into their daily lives, positively impacting other areas of their life and helping them develop focus, self-discipline, and mindfulness.

3. **Surrender and Submission:** Islamic prayer is an act of surrender and submission to Allah's (SWT) will. During prayer, Muslims acknowledge that they depend on Allah (SWT), recognizing that only His allag hold the ultimate control. Prayer teaches worshippers to let go of their desires, ego, and attachments and embrace surrender to the Divine will.

4. **Spiritual Revitalization and Renewal:** Islamic prayer is also a way of spiritually revitalizing and renewing oneself. It is a sanctuary, providing shelter from the distractions and chaos of life and allowing worshippers to connect with their inner selves, allowing their spiritual energy to rejuvenate. Because worshippers are focused on remembering Allah (SWT), their hearts and souls are revitalized, giving a sense of spiritual nourishment.

5. **Connection to the Prophet:** Islamic prayer isn't just about developing a connection to Allah (SWT); it's also about following the Prophet Muhammad's (PBUH) examples and teachings. His life serves as a guide to Muslims in every aspect of their life, including prayer. Muslims use their prayers to emulate his humility,

sincerity, and devotion, thus strengthening the connection and giving their spiritual journey more depth.

6. **Transcending the Material World:** Muslims try to transcend the material world during prayer, raising their consciousness as near to the divine realm as possible. During prayer, they detach from their concerns and focus only on Allah (SWT), experiencing spiritual transcendence. This gives them a clearer perspective in life and helps them find purpose and solace beyond the material world.

7. **Growth and Transformation:** The act of praying is transformative, allowing for spiritual development and personal growth. By engaging in prayer regularly, worshippers can develop gratitude, patience, self-discipline, compassion, and other similar virtues. Islamic prayer encourages self-improvement and self-reflection, not to mention purification of character, which all leads to continued spiritual growth.

8. **Mindfulness and Presence:** Islamic prayer also strongly emphasizes being mindful and present during worship. Muslims are encouraged to be focused on their thoughts, with complete concentration on what the recitations mean, and be fully engaged in remembering Allah (SWT) with their hearts and souls. Developing mindfulness allows them to have a deeper Divine connection and develop a stronger spiritual awareness.

9. **Integrating Faith into Their Daily Lives:** The spiritual journey of prayer goes beyond the time spent praying. It continually guides Muslims through daily life, influencing their choices and decisions and helping them embody Islamic teachings and values. The spiritual insights they get from prayer help them work through

ethical and moral dilemmas, make good choices, and remain consciously aware of their responsibilities and actions.

10. **Self-Reflection and Inner Dialogue:** Praying gives Muslims time to self-reflect and have an inner dialogue. As they stand before Allah (SWT), they converse with Him, telling him of their fears, hopes, and gratitude and asking for guidance. Introspection allows them to develop self-awareness and a deep understanding of their emotions, thoughts, and spiritual needs.

11. **Spiritual Enlightenment and Divine Guidance:** All Muslims believe that Islamic prayer helps them channel spiritual enlightenment and divine guidance. With sincere supplications and requests for guidance from Allah (SWT), they open themselves up to clarity and wisdom and gain important insights into their lives. They believe that Allah (SWT) responds to all His servants' prayers and gives them the enlightenment and guidance they need.

12. **Spiritual Healing and Emotional Release:** Islamic prayer allows worshippers to express their deepest worries, emotions, and desires before Allah (SWT). When they can share this with Him and use prayer to seek solace, they experience emotional release, spiritual healing, and comfort. Prayer is their sacred space; it's where they go to seek solace in the Divine presence and gain the strength they need to overcome the challenges that come their way.

To finish, I want to share a story with you to illustrate the spiritual journey of Islamic prayer.

There was once a young Muslim man who struggled to cope with feelings of confusion and emptiness. His life was successful in material terms, but his heart was empty. He needed answers, so he turned to Islamic prayer, praying regularly and with deep sincerity.

As he prayed, he began to experience something he had never felt before – clarity and peace. The solitude of prayer allowed him to reflect on his intentions, actions, and aspirations in life. He began to realize that he had lost the connection to this spiritual essence in his pursuit of the material world and wealth.

He began to build a connection to Allah (SWT), asking for His forgiveness, mercy, and guidance. In telling Allah (SWT) of his hopes, worries, and dreams, he found great comfort, and the more he prayed, the deeper his connection became.

Over time, he changed his perspective on life, and prayer was no longer a physical act; it became a journey, a way to purify himself and embark on a path of self-improvement. He realized that prayer was more than just ritual; it was an open doorway to higher consciousness and a deep connection to Allah (SWT).

That is what all Muslims strive for, and Islamic prayer is a big part of their spiritual journey, perhaps one of the most important, as it teaches them how to live their lives in spiritual fulfillment.

Conclusion

Thank you for taking the time to read my guide. I hope you now better understand Islamic prayer and its importance to those who follow the Muslim faith. Here's how we broke this guide down into easy chapters to help you understand everything:

Chapter 1 discussed the concept of prayer in Islam and why it is so important. We learned a bit about the Islamic prayer's history and briefly discussed the five Islamic pillars.

In Chapter 2, we looked at the significance of prayer and its spiritual, physical, and emotional benefits before moving on to using prayer to connect with Allah (SWT).

Chapter 3 discussed the rituals and requirements of prayer. We started with the five daily prayers before looking at the requirements. This includes preparing oneself mentally, physically, and emotionally before doing a cleansing ritual. This ritual is known as Wudu, and full steps were provided on how to do it. We also provided full steps on how to pray, including positions for each part, and prayers were also included for you to practice with.

Chapter 4 gave you a brief overview of the components of Islamic prayer, while Chapter 5 discussed ways to enhance the quality of your Salah to achieve a deeper, more meaningful connection.

Chapter 6 put some common misconceptions to bed and answered some questions, while Chapter 7 looked at overcoming challenges in prayer by learning focus and deep concentration.

In Chapter 8, we discussed the importance of praying five times daily and finished with Chapter 9, where we discussed prayer as a spiritual journey.

This guide should have given you a good idea of Salah, and you should now understand why it is so important to the Muslim faith and why it is so important in their daily lives.

I hope you now have everything you need to understand the importance of prayer in Islam. Please consider leaving a review at Amazon.com if you found this book useful.

References

Beginner's Guide to Learning How to Pray Salah. (n.d.). My Masjid. https://www.mymasjid.ca/beginners-guide-learn-pray-salah/

Constituent Parts of Prayer. (n.d.). Al Islam. https://www.alislam.org/book/salat/constituent-parts-of-prayer/

How to Perform Prayer (Salah). (n.d.). Dar Al-Iftaa. https://www.dar-alifta.org/en/article/details/250/how-to-perform-prayer-salah

أحمد, ريس‏‏. "Significance of Prayer." *IslamOnline*, 18 Dec. 2022, islamonline.net/en/significance-of-prayer/.

"10 Misconceptions about Islam - IslamiCity." *Www.islamicity.org*, www.islamicity.org/11238/10-misconceptions-about-islam/.

"Chapter 5 - the 5 Daily Salah - Masjid Ar-Rahmah | Mosque of Mercy." *Www.mymasjid.ca*, www.mymasjid.ca/beginners-guide-learn-pray-salah/chapter-5.

Goraya, Azhar. "Why Muslims Pray 5 Times a Day." *Review of Religions*, 26 Feb. 2020, www.reviewofreligions.org/20026/why-muslims-pray-5-times-a-day/.

"How Do Muslims Pray? A Short History of Prayer in Islam." *Raseef22*, 22 Nov. 2016, raseef22.net/english/article/1068061-muslims-pray-short-history-prayer-islam.

islamonline_en. "Introduction to How to Perform Salah (1)." *IslamOnline*, 23 Oct. 2021, islamonline.net/en/introduction-to-how-to-perform-salah-1/.

Muslimhowto. *How to Dress for Salat.* www.muslimhowto.com/2020/03/how-to-dress-for-salat.html.

Newton, Colin. "Strategies for Concentrating in Prayer." *Inclusive Solutions*, 14 June 2021, inclusive-solutions.com/blog/strategies-for-concentrating-in-prayer/#:~:text=Indeed%2C%20taking%20charge%20of%20your.

"Prayer in Islam." *The British Library*, www.bl.uk/sacred-texts/articles/prayer-in-islam#:~:text=In%20Islam%2C%20prayer%2C%20supplication%2C.

Quran Explorer. "Quran - Recite & Listen Quran Online." *Www.quranexplorer.com*, www.quranexplorer.com/blog/Education-In-The-Light-Of-Sunnah-And-Qura.

Quran Academy. "How to Improve the Quality of Your Salah." *Quran Academy*, quranacademy.io/blog/improve-quality-of-your-salah/.

Printed in Great Britain
by Amazon

43907413R00076